# MARIJUANA CHEMISTRY

## Genetics, Processing, & Potency

by Michael Starks

Ronin Publishing, Inc.
P.O.Box 1035 Berkeley, CA 94701

Published by
Ronin Publishing, Inc.
Post Office Box 1035
Berkeley, California 94701

MARIJUANA CHEMISTRY
ISBN: 0-914171-39-9
Copyright © 1977 & 1990 by Michael Starks
(Originally published by And/Or Press, inc. as *Marijuana Potency*)

Editors: Sebastian Orfali, Candice Jacobson
Production: Sebastian Orfali, Meda Matrix, Paulette Traverso
Photograph credits: pp104-108 by Irimias the Obscure;
        pp 2, 88, 103, 126 by Harlan A. Reiders; p 16 by Lew Watts.
Chemical structures on pp 7, 8, and 9 reprinted with permission from
        R. Mechoulam, *Marijuana* (Academic Press, New York, 1973).
Appendix on chemical synthesis reprinted with permission from
        Michael V. Smith, *Psychedelic Chemistry* (Rip-Off Press, 1973).
Illustration on page 49 reprinted with permission from
        Joyce & Curry, *Botany and Chemistry of Cannabis* (Churchill &
        Livingston: Edinburgh, 1970). Ilustration by D. Erasmus.

U.S. Library of Congress Catalog Number: 77-82454
Printed in the United States of America
4th printing, March 1995

# Introduction
# to
# Second Edition

Reviewing the work on the botany and chemistry of marijuana which has appeared in the twelve years since the publication of the first edition of this work is both gratifying and dismaying. It is gratifying in that the conclusions reached earlier are in need of no significant revision and dismaying in that they have been largely ignored. It is amazing that so little work has been done on such a fundamental issue as the effect of cannabidiol on the high and other actions of THC and that when studies on the high finally appeared they were done by Brazilians! Probably the red tape involved in doing research on humans with psychedelics is a major barrier. I am reminded of the failure of nearly thirty years of research to determine the influence of iso-LSD on the LSD experience. Likewise, only a few of the hundreds of THC and LSD homologs and analogs have been adequately tested for psychoactivity. Only a trickle of work has appeared on the promising marijuana clones. Also, no attempt seems to have been made to reinstate hemp fiber as a significant source of paper, rope and cloth, in spite of the beautiful examples of hemp and hemp-cotton cloth still available from Japan. The history and use of hemp fiber has hardly been touched upon in the modern English literature and all the great classic works in other languages remain untranslated. Finally, my suggestions on the necessity of measuring the total cannabinoid content of plants in order to eliminate the spurious fluctuations due to other constituents have gone unheeded.

Clearly, there remains a considerable amount of work for researchers.

I have chosen to place the new material as an addendum so as to enable the many readers of the first edition to immediately acquaint themselves with the progress in the field.

Michael Starks
Berkeley, California
January, 1990

# Preface

In the last few years it has become possible to approach the question of marijuana potency in a rational manner for the first time. This is mainly due to the widespread application of modern analytical techniques such as thin layer and gas chromatography to plant analysis. I have attempted here the first general survey of the scientific results relative to the high produced by smoking or eating various marijuana preparations. Sophisticated users can now gauge roughly what effects a given sample will have simply by learning its tetrahydrocannibinol and cannabidiol contents. Furthermore, if they know the origin of the seeds, they will know a great deal about the probable potency of the resulting plants.

I have tried to summarize a vast amount of complicated data in a fashion comprehensible to the general reader. Consequently, I have sometimes simplified the information and have included only a few key references of the hundreds examined. Nevertheless, I have tried to be accurate and would appreciate any corrections or comments from readers.

The author wishes to thank Candice Jacobson for an exhaustive job of copyediting.

# Contents

# MARIJUANA CHEMISTRY
## Genetics, Processing, & Potency

# Abbreviations

CBD     cannabidiol
CBDA   cannabidiolic acid
CBN     cannabinol
CBDV   cannabidivarol
THCV   tetrahydrocannabivarol
THC     tetrahydrocannabinol
THCA   tetrahydrocannabinolic acid

# Introduction

Psychoactive plants have had an extremely important position in most societies. Consumption of such plants tens or even hundreds of thousands of years ago may have been responsible for generating much of the mythology and religion, indeed, much of the very fabric of culture which so strikingly distinguishes man from even the most advanced of the great apes. Could it be that these plants provided sparks to kindle the flame of intellect which now shines so brightly it threatens to destroy the world? Countless millions of times priests, elders and sages consumed potent preparations of psychoactive plants in order to attune themselves to nature and act in accordance with natural or divine law. This is still done in many of the less technologically evolved societies. The almost universal occurrence of such practices (or their substitutes such as meditation, yoga, trance, hypnosis) testifies to their effectiveness. Western Europe, however, was largely devoid of such plants and consequently of traditions for using them to put oneself in harmony with the surroundings. American traditions have mostly evolved from those of Western Europe and this is one reason for considerable resistance to the use of psychedelic drugs.

Most of the psychoactive plants contain large amounts of alkaloids. These are bitter tasting, nitrogen containing bases which have a wide variety of effects on animals. Why do so many plants contain chemicals that have striking actions on animal nervous systems? Surely the chemicals or some closely related chemicals found in the plants must play important roles in the economy of the plant or else the many genes required for their synthesis would be eliminated by natural selection. In view of the fundamental similarity of all living organisms, it is not surprising that all of them contain chemicals which are active on all the others. Nevertheless, the relatively high concentrations of many psychoactive substances are still puzzling and their precise functions in the plants remain a mystery.

The active chemicals of marijuana, though they are unusual in that they are not alkaloids, do not contain nitrogen and are relatively insoluble in water, likewise have no known reason for being in the plant. However, the psychoactive constituents of *Cannabis* are unusual, in fact unique, in that they are largely produced in specialized groups of cells termed lactifers, stalked glands and sessile (i.e., not stalked) glands, and in their being released from these cells to form a sticky coating. This will be discussed in more detail later in chapter one.

Before delving into the basic chemistry of *Cannabis,* a few words of explanation for those unfamiliar with organic chemistry are appropriate. C, H, O, and N refer respectively to atoms of carbon, hydrogen, oxygen and nitrogen. R indicates that a number of different chemical groups (radicals) may occur at this position. In accordance with common conventions, carbon and hydrogen atoms are often omitted in structural formulas. Thus, delta-one-tetrahydrocannabinol shown in figure one actually has 21 carbon atoms and 30 hydrogen atoms. A single line between two atoms indicates a single bond (single pair of shared electrons) while a double line indicates a double bond (two pairs of shared electrons). A double bond is said to be unsaturated because hydrogen or other atoms can be added to it, as when cannabidiol is converted by the plant to THC. Conversely, atoms may be removed from single bonds to produce double bonds as when THC converts to CBN (see figure one). Carbon always has four bonds.

Do not be put off by the chemical formulas and detailed tables in this book—they are absolutely necessary for an adequate understanding of marijuana potency and can be understood by anyone willing to spend a few hours reading. The rewards for making the effort are substantial—you will have a rational, scientific basis for buying, growing, harvesting, storing, preparing, testing and using marijuana and hashish.

# 1

# Marijuana Constituents and Their Effects

## Cannabinoids— The Active Chemicals of Marijuana

Although chemical research on marijuana began over 150 years ago, it wasn't until 1964 that the first authenticated isolation of a pure, active principle delta-one tetrahydrocannabinol ($\Delta^1$-THC) was achieved, and not until 1970 that it was determined to be the only major psychoactive component. Even though dozens of cannabinoids have been isolated since then, none have been found to be significantly psychoactive.

Cannabinoids are the compounds with 21 carbon atoms; they and their carboxylic acids, analogs and transformation products are some of the chemical components of marijuana. Figures 1, 2 and 3 give the structures of a few of these compounds and their probable biosynthetic relationships. Most cannabinoids are extremely insoluble in water, and in the living cell they are probably present entirely as their carboxylic acids. When isolated from fresh marijuana they are usually in their acid form until aging, drying and heat decarboxylate them. The data usually give the percentage of weight of cannabinoids in their neutral form, decarboxylated. The acids are not biologically active, but this is only important if marijuana is eaten or injected, since smoking decarboxylates them. Most marijuana seems to contain largely or exclusively the "A" form of the acids (shown in figure 2), but variants have been observed which have some of the "B" form. One Indian variant contained ten times as much "A" as "B" and one hashish sample had very little "A." These positional isomers have not been investigated much and their significance is unknown.

$\Delta^{1(6)}$-THC (shown in figure 2) is a minor constituent of

marijuana, seldom exceeding more than a few percent of the
$\Delta^1$-THC content and having about the same biological activity.
It has been suspected of being an artifact of marijuana extrac-
tion and analysis.

The biosynthetic route of the cannabinoids (the biochemical pathways by which they are synthesized in the living plant)
has not been fully worked out, but the most probable routes are
given in figure 3. Starting from precursors such as isoprene or
mevalonic acid, compounds of the olivetolic acid and geranyl
pyrophosphate type are condensed via intermediates such as cannabigerolic acid to give cannabidiolic acid, which is cyclized to
give tetrahydrocannabinolic acid. Time and heat will subsequently cause a certain amount of the THC acid to be dehydrogenated
to cannabinolic acid or cannabinol (CBN). At some point, THC
and /or cannabidiol (CBD) are extruded through the cell membrane. Whether this happens continually or only after a critical
concentration has been reached has not been established: polymers of THC may be formed at this time, but their amounts and
possible contribution to marijuana activity have not been investigated.

A great deal of research has been directed at determining
the activity of the various chemical constituents of marijuana.
One study used the three main compounds, THC, CBD (the biosynthetic precursor to THC) and CBN (the immediate degrada-
tion product of THC). The researchers injected measured
amounts of each of the compounds in pure form intravenously
in human subjects. For THC, it was found that 20 mcg per kilogram of body weight was the average minimum amount per-
ceived to induce a high, while 50 mcg per kilogram was the average maximum amount desired. For CBN these figures were 200
and 270 mcg per kilogram respectively, while for CBD, no high
was reported even at 270 mcg per kilogram. However, recent
studies show that CBD, while having no direct effect by itself,
can have a significant interaction with THC.[1]

# The Cannabidiol Story

The widely varying effects of marijuana and hashish have long

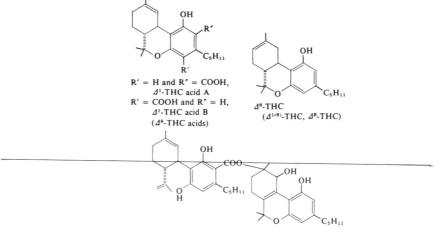

R = H, Cannabidiol (CBD)
R = COOH,
   Cannabidiolic acid

$\Delta^1$-Tetrahydrocannabinol, (R = H)
$\Delta^1$-THC ($\Delta^9$-THC)
$\Delta^1$-Tetrahydrocannabinolic acid
  (R = COOH)

R = H, Cannabinol (CBN)
R = COOH, Cannabinolic acid

$\Delta^1$-Tetrahydrocannabivarol
(tetrahydrocannabidivarol,
tetrahydrocannabivarin,
propyl-THC)

Cannabivarol
(cannabidivarol,
cannabivarin,
propyl cannabinol)

Cannabidivarol
(cannabidivarin,
propyl cannabidiol)

Fig. 1. Some naturally occurring cannabinoids. The top three compounds are by far the most important, with the set of three compounds below being identical except that the side chain is shortened by 2 carbon atoms in the cannabidivarol series. Later in the text look for a discussion of the series with the propyl side chain, and see the Appendix for the numbering system used. (Reprinted, by permission, from R. Mechoulam, *Marijuana*, 1973.)

R' = H and R" = COOH,
  $\Delta^1$-THC acid A
R' = COOH and R" = H,
  $\Delta^1$-THC acid B
  ($\Delta^9$-THC acids)

$\Delta^6$-THC
($\Delta^{1(6)}$-THC, $\Delta^8$-THC)

Fig. 2. Other naturally occurring cannabinoids. (Reprinted, by permission, from R. Mechoulam, *Marijuana*, 1973.)

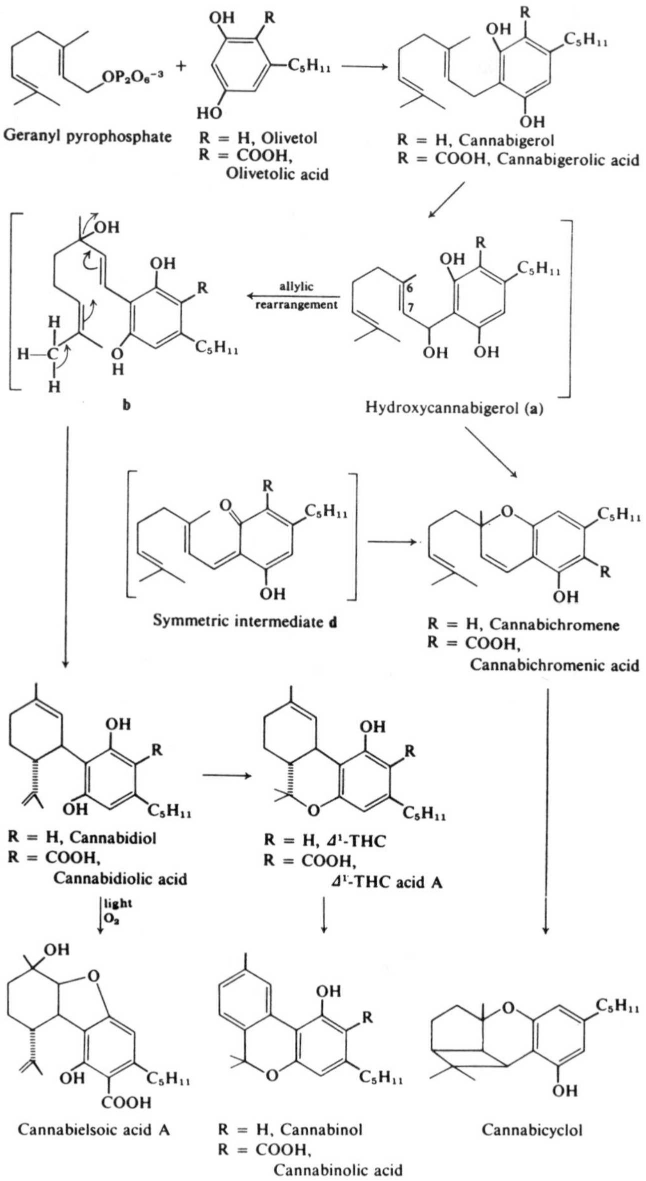

Fig. 3. Probable biosynthetic relationships of the major cannabinoids. (Reprinted, by permission, from R. Mechoulam, *Marijuana,* 1973.)

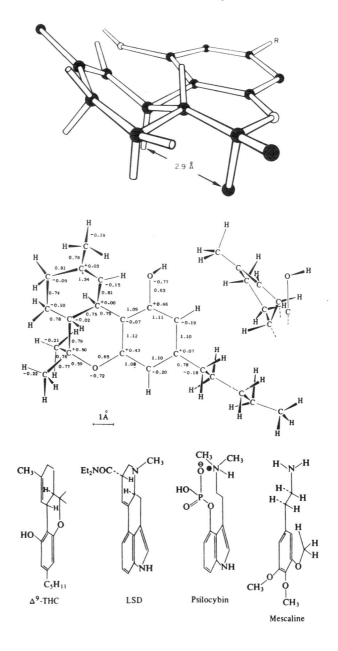

Fig. 4. Structural aspects of THC. (Reprinted, by permission, from R. Mechoulam, *Marijuana*, 1973.)

puzzled researchers. If THC is the only psychoactive component, one should get high in proportion to the percentage of
THC, especially since studies have shown that pure THC produces essentially the same effects as marijuana. However, the
fact is that different samples produce a qualitatively different
type of high and that heavy THC content (as in many samples
of hashish) does not guarantee a good high. Recent scientific
research is helping us to make sense out of this.

The only compounds that may have effects themselves or
may affect the response to THC are CBD and CBN. These two
compounds have relatively minor sedative effects in the amounts
in which they are likely to be ingested or smoked by ordinary
users. Recent studies have shown that they tend to increase the
depressant effects of THC while blocking its excitant effects.
That is, they tend to make the user sleepy and block the high.
The actual situation is more subtle: CBN can synergise with
THC to increase mental effects, but CBN will seldom be of consequence in natural situations since it is not usually present in
high concentrations and has low potency. Another possibility is
that CBD may decrease the depressant effects of THC as well as
the excitant effects. Usually, however, as in a recent experiment
in which subjects smoked THC with and without CBD (at six
times the THC amount) the CBD significantly decreased the
euphoria of THC while having no effect itself. When CBD was
taken with THC orally at two times the THC amount, it delayed
the onset but extended the duration of the high.

The practical conclusions of these findings seem to be:
(1) the CBD content of marijuana and hashish should be as low
as possible in order to get a good high; (2) a high THC content
only means a good high if accompanied by a low CBD content;
(3) any grass containing lots of CBD should be extracted and the
CBD isomerized to THC; (4) careful evaluation of grass requires
quantitative testing for THC and CBD content.

The effects of CBD on the THC high need further investiga-
tion, however. It is possible that when present in large amounts,
CBD is involved in some of the interesting and pleasurable as-
pects of the high. It may well be that marijuana that has lots of
CBD and THC can be more desirable than that with THC alone.
This may be why hashish, though it normally has much less THC

than CBD, is frequently a better high than one would expect on the basis of THC content alone.

This could also explain some of the striking differences in subjective experience afforded by different marijuana. As the CBD content increases relative to that of THC, the high will be weakened and delayed. Thus, grass which has an adequate THC content (say 1%) but significant amounts of CBD (say 0.5%) will tend to be very mild, but will slowly creep up on the user and may have him more stoned four hours later than if there were no CBD present. Sometimes this is advantageous; in a recent experiment naïve subjects reported that joints containing CBD with THC were more pleasant than with THC alone. The CBD attenuated the high enough to rid them of anxiety and the jitters.[2]

Hopefully, it is now clear why the various tables include both THC and CBD. Getting high is becoming a science as well as an art. By paying careful attention to the tables and correlating them with personal experience, it may eventually be possible to judge fairly closely the nature of the high obtainable from a given marijuana sample. Simple, rapid chemical tests for home use will soon be available for the determination of THC and CBD content. Merely knowing the origin of the seeds can also give a good gauge for evaluating the quality of the resulting marijuana crop, regardless of where it is being grown. Of course, differences in seeds, growth conditions and age will still produce considerable variation, but seeds from high THC plants will usually grow into high THC plants.

To summarize, the cannabidiol story is confusing because of the complex nature of its interactions with THC and because relatively little research has been done. Meanwhile, it seems reasonable to assume that as CBD content approaches that of THC, the high will be diminished in intensity, but prolonged.

## Smoking Versus Eating

It's more efficient to smoke than eat—at least if you are trying to get high. Most of the data on smoking is derived from analysis of condensates from cigarette smoking machines, and it is unclear whether the results are equivalent to what one would get from people smoking. But the results indicate at least 20% (and a maximum of 60%) of the THC present in a joint reaches the lungs, with the amount increasing to perhaps 45% when the same substance is smoked in a pipe. An experienced smoker who inhales deeply and holds it in a long time will retain up to 80% of the cannabinoids inhaled.

The main chemical change upon smoking seems to be decarboxylation of THC acid to THC. This is particularly important for fresh, moist samples in which the THC will not be active and will need decarboxylation. Other samples which have been heated or stored awhile normally have had the THC decarboxylated already. Smoking also converts some of the THC into the inactive CBN and produces in small amounts a number of other compounds of minor significance. Smoking does not cause much cyclization of CBD to THC unless the marijuana is mixed with tobacco (common in most areas except the U.S.), and even then only a small amount of such cyclization may occur.

When pure, THC is roughly three times more potent when smoked than when eaten. Smoking about 6 mg, or eating about 15 mg, of THC will feel like a minimal high to most people; whereas smoking 30 mg or eating 75 mg will tend to produce very intense effects, comparable to those from LSD. However, when hashish or marijuana is eaten, it may be five or ten times less potent than smoking due to incomplete absorption from the intenstine. In terms of average marijuana containing 1% THC, this would mean that smoking roughly 1 gram would provide a minimal high, a condition also obtainable by eating 3 grams. Don't forget that most THC is present in the orally inactive acid form. Consequently it should first be finely pulverized and well-baked in an oven in order to decarboxylate the acid.

What about water pipes? A recent experiment showed that the water soluble substances absorbed in the water pipe were inactive. This is as expected, since cannabinoids are insoluble in water. However, the insoluble material that collected on the top of the water and on the walls of the pipe was very active. Relative to a condensate of the smoke which reaches the lungs, it contained 1/3 the THC, 1/4 the CBD, and slightly more CBN. Some water pipe devotees use wine in their pipes (cherry wine is my favorite) and a small percentage of cannabinoids may be expected to dissolve in the alcohol. However, as the pipe is used, the alcohol will gradually steam distill. When the alcoholic content drops, the cannabinoids will precipitate on the bottom and walls. Water pipes have the advantage of cooling the smoke; while there is greater efficiency in smoking a joint, water pipes also filter out large particles and are probably easier on the lungs.[3]

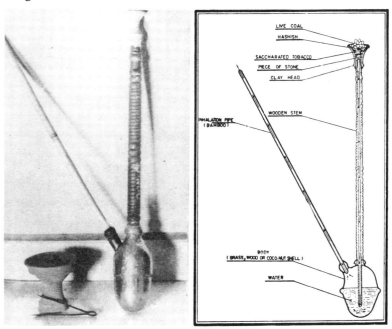

Fig. 5. Middle Eastern water pipe. Typical of Egypt and adjacent countries, water pipes of this sort have been used for about 400 years. The hashish typically rests on a layer of tobacco (saccharated, sugared in this example) and is ignited with live coals from the chafing dish. The smoke passing down the stem is cooled and filtered by the water. (Reprinted from M. Soueif, *Bulletin on Narcotics*, 1967.)

## Deterioration

Hashish deteriorates with time. In India it is stored only for about three years. After that, it loses its dark brown or greenish color and resinous quality, becoming brownish-grey, hard and crumbly. This loss of potency is due to oxidation; the center of a chunk will remain potent longer than the outside. Raphael

Mechoulam, the pioneer marijuana experimenter, found one chunk of hash with 2% THC on the outside, but 8% inside. Twenty years earlier, marijuana researcher Levine found that after three years a 100-pound lump of *charas* (hashish) had retained its potency in the center, while the crust contained 1/20 of its former potency.

In India, *ganja* (flowering tops) is generally considered useless by the end of two years, while the *bhang* (leaves), which have a lower THC content, are said to be fairly stable and may keep for three or four years. During the fourth year, however, they are prized mainly as a cooling and soothing drink rather than for their intoxicating quality.

The ratio between the amount of CBN (the decomposition product of THC) and the total amount of cannabinoids can be used to determine the approximate age of a sample. One study found that under tropical conditions in India, the ratio of CBN to CBN plus THC increased about 12% per year for *charas* and 3.5% per year for *ganja.* The smaller the ratio, the more recent the sample. Hashish deteriorates faster than *ganja* because it is more exposed to air during manufacture.

The importance of the intactness was shown in a recent British study. There was about twice as much loss of THC over a year's time if the marijuana was passed through a 0.33 mm mesh than if a 1 mm mesh was used; the experiment was conducted in a dark room kept at 20° C. Even so, the yearly loss in the more finely powdered samples varied from 16 to 43%, for unknown reasons. The effect of light was also significant over a one-year period. The decrease in THC was 36% in the light versus 13% in the dark. Light has a greater effect on manicured marijuana than on intact material.

One of the best studies on the deterioration of marijuana with time was reported in 1973 by University of Mississippi researchers. They put dried, manicured marijuana in amber glass bottles which were not airtight and observed cannabinoid content at various temperatures for 100 weeks. The following table gives the results. Note that 76° F is approximately room temperature and 98° F is near normal body temperature of 98.6° F.

Table 1 shows that if marijuana is stored for a year at room temperature in the dark, it should not lose more than about

10% in potency. The CBD content was constant at all temperatures. As is usually the case with fresh marijuana, most of the THC (about 95%) was actually present as THC acid. Significant decarboxylation of THC acid to THC occurred only at 98° F, when it decarboxylated about 50% during the year period. An experiment on hashish showed that one minute at 50° C (122° F) decarboxylated about 50% of the THC acid. Thus, a few minutes in a 200° F oven would suffice for complete conversion, and would render all the THC in the sample orally active.

Clearly, the more the plant structure is disrupted, the more rapid the THC loss will be. If the plant is harvested without being manicured (seeds and stems removed), expect somewhat less THC loss than indicated in table 1. If it is finely crushed or run through a sieve, somewhat more loss can be expected. Also, there is no need to store marijuana in the refrigerator unless you live in an area where the temperature will consistently exceed 90° F *and* you plan to store it longer than a year. It is true that if not dried properly, marijuana might get moldy, especially if kept in plastic bags, and that in time the cannabinoids will break down and potency decrease. Contrary to popular belief, moldy marijuana is less potent than dry. But, like the myths of potency increase with dry ice treatment, speed in acid, and brain damage from DMT, this belief will probably never die.

If you are concerned with achieving the least potency loss, it is best to store your marijuana, uncleaned, in an airtight container in a dark, cool place. Since it takes a considerable amount of time for the potency to decrease, this will give you the option of not smoking certain marijuana for a period of time and then returning to it assured that its potency is undiminished.[4]

## TABLE 1
## MARIJUANA POTENCY
## DECREASE WITH AGE

| TEMPERATURE | | YEARLY |
|---|---|---|
| °F | °C | % THC LOST |
| 0 | -18 | 3.8 |
| 39 | 4 | 5.4 |
| 76 | 22 | 6.9 |
| 98 | 37 | ⌣20.0 |

# 2

# Growth Conditions and Potency

## Species

There is currently much confusion about the number of species in the genus *Cannabis*. Some botanists hold that, on the basis of morphological criteria, there are three species: *sativa, indica* and *ruderalis*. These are characterized as follows: (Note that *akenes*—often spelled *achenes*—is the technically correct name for seeds. The abscission layer is the site where the seed is attached.)

*C. sativa:* Plants usually tall (five to eighteen feet), laxly branched. Akenes smooth, usually lacking marbled pattern of outer coat, firmly attached to stalk and without definite articulation.

*C. indica:* Plants usually small (four feet or less), not laxly branched. Akenes usually marbled on outer coat, with definite abscission layer, dropping off at maturity. Plants very densely branched, more or less conical, usually four feet tall or less. Abscission layer a simple articulation at base of akene.

*C. ruderalis:* Plants not branched or very sparsely so, usually one or two feet at maturity. Abscission layer forms a fleshy caruncle-like growth at base of akene.

    *C. ruderalis* is a wild species which occurs as a weed in cultivated fields in southeastern Russia and central Asia, and is spreading westward into Europe. It does not occur in the USA. It is also distinguished by its extremely short leaves and seeds that tend to be smaller than *C. sativa* seeds (akenes). *C. indica* tends to have small, almost spherical seeds, averaging smaller than those of *C. ruderalis* and generally has alternate leaves, in contrast to *C. sativa*, which tends to have opposite leaves. *C. sativa* seeds are often highly compressed longitudinally so that when pressure is applied to the peripheral ridges, they easily fall apart, in contrast to those of *C. indica*. *C. sativa* seeds are the largest of the three species, often exceeding 5 mm in length. *C. sativa* tends to have very narrow leaflets, while *C. indica* usually has much broader ones.

Crossing experiments with 38 different strains from around the world showed normal meiosis, completely strainable pollen, high pollen fertility, and no chromosomal aberrations. This indicates that there are no fertility barriers between the species. However, *C. ruderalis* and the true wild ancestral populations from central Asia (the putative "home" of *Cannabis*) have not been tested. Regardless of the results, fertility barriers are not the criterion for species determination; rather the criteria lie in the delineation of consistent (hereditary) morphological or physiological variations. Much further study of wild ancestral populations from central Asia (if they exist) is needed to settle this question. In view of the prolonged viability of frozen seeds, it may be possible to germinate seeds frozen in the arctic for thousands of years and get a look at truly wild ancestral hemp.

Fig. 6. Type specimens of the names *Cannabis sativa* L. (left) and *C. indica* Lam. (center) and putative type of the name *C. ruderalis* Jan. (right). A type specimen is the original specimen on which the scientific description of a species is based. The "L" after *Cannabis sativa* stands for Linnaeus, whose *Systema Plantarum* (1753) is the starting point for scientific names of plants. (Reprinted from Small, *Plant Science Bulletin,* vol. 35, 1975.)

It would be of special interest to find out whether a particular chemical, especially a cannabinoid, occurs in one of the putative species, but not in the others. The limited data thus far available do not afford much hope in this respect. Four or five stocks designated *ruderalis* have all been of the high CBD, low THC type, but further investigation will probably reveal, as with the other two supposed species, that high, low and intermediate levels of each cannabinoid can be discovered in some stocks. Thus far nobody has been able to correlate any morphological difference with a chemical difference between species.[1]

The cultivation of marijuana may extend back 10,000 years or more, but unlike many other cultivated plants (e.g., tomatoes, potatoes, corn), it has never been totally domesticated. It easily escapes to become a naturalized weed. The effects of breeding for oil, fiber and THC content, coupled with continual escape and crossing with wild or naturalized populations has led to extreme variability which blurs specific differences.

Finally, it should be noted that some botanists, and the law, maintain that there is only one species. If this view prevails, the above "species" will have the status of subspecies or cultivated varieties (cultivars).

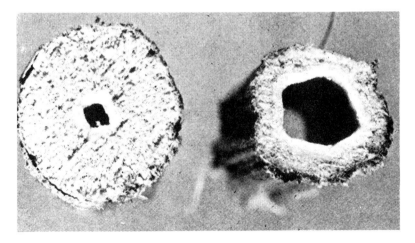

Fig. 7. Cross sections of stems at internodes of a low THC fiber variant (left) and of a high THC variant (right). Fiber varieties have hollower stems at the internodes, allowing more energy to be directed into the production of fibers in the phloem. (Reprinted from Small, *Plant Science Bulletin,* vol. 35, 1975.)

# Seeds

In addition to the differences between the seeds of the "species" noted above, there seem to be consistent differences between wild and cultivated seeds of each type. Wild seeds tend to be smaller, with comparatively well-developed abscission zones, narrow bases, and a papery layer (perianth) of marbled or mottled appearance. Germination is slow and irregular. All these characteristics are thought to be of survival value in nature. Wild plants will often have minimal energy for seed production, making numerous small seeds an obvious selective advantage. Likewise, the narrow bases and well-developed abscission zones help to facilitate dispersal, while the marbled coat might provide protection or camouflage against seed eaters. Slow, erratic germination will be desirable where water availability may be irregular, particularly during the first months of the growing season. Many, if not most, wild populations have only recently escaped from cultivation. They show the above characteristics to varying degrees, influenced by the continual escape of drug and fiber strains to interbreed with them.

It should be pointed out, however, that there is also considerable variation among seeds of both cultivated and wild strains. A recent study found that wild populations in southern Asia, especially India, were largely lacking the marbled perianth, while most wild Chinese seeds were rather large and had no adhering perianth or base elongation—thus resembling the cultivated seeds. Many cultivated seeds have the marbled perianth, but it usually sloughs off easily and seldom persists on the mature seed.

One generalization which *can* be made about marijuana seeds is that they can survive for extremely long periods if conditions are right. And there are a variety of "right" conditions. One Japanese scientist found high germination rates in seeds kept dry with calcium chloride for 14 years. Another (American) study of fiber type hemp seeds found that low temperatures were the most important factor: better than 95% of seeds kept for eight years, stored in cloth bags or sealed jars, germinated when the temperature was maintained at 10° C or less. Seeds kept in a freezer maintain viability quite well.

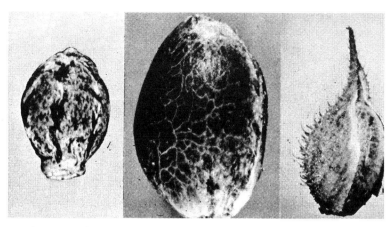

Fig. 8. Seed of *Cannabis.* At extreme right, a seed still hooded by its bract is shown. (X6). At extreme left is the seed of a wild plant, and in the center, of a domesticated plant (both X9). Note that the wild seed is smaller, has an attenuated base, an obvious abscission zone at the base, and is covered with a marbled papery material (perianth). (Reprinted from Small, *Plant Science Bulletin,* vol. 35, 1975.)

Drying of seeds seems to make very little difference until higher temperatures are reached. At 21° C (70° F), seeds conditioned to 6.2% moisture showed no decreased germination after five years, but seeds conditioned to 9.5% (about the normal moisture content) showed only 5% germination after two years. However, when exposed to normal ambient temperatures in unheated buildings, seeds do not survive as well. When stored in sealed jars in Kentucky or Maryland, germination was down to about 40% after three years, but in the cooler climate of Washington, there was no significant drop in six years. It seems quite possible that if seeds were kept frozen or at low temperatures, they might last for centuries. This would be especially true for wild seeds, which last much longer on the average, than the cultivated varieties. (All of the above data were gathered on seeds of the cultivated fiber type of *C. sativa.)*

To sum up, seeds will keep very well in sealed jars if the jars are stored in a cool place such as a refrigerator or freezer. But even in sealed jars, if they are frequently exposed to temperatures above 50° or 60° F, they will show a marked decline in germination within two years and will be mostly or entirely sterile within four; at least this is true for the high CBD type seeds in northern latitudes. These germination rates cannot, however, be expected for seeds from commercial marijuana, where the seeds have often been crushed or not allowed to fully ripen.[2]

It is possible, by selective pollination, to obtain seeds which yield all (or nearly all) males or females. This can be done by crossing with certain monoecious strains, or by a simpler method available to almost anyone. If the male flowers that arise on a female plant are used as the pollen source, the resulting seeds will all be females. If the plant does not do this naturally, there are various techniques for inducing the monoecious conditions, such as low light, low night temperatures, stress, and spraying with Ethrel. These techniques will be discussed in more detail in future chapters.

## Function of Cannabinoids in Marijuana

It is commonly believed that the function of the resin secreted by marijuana is to prevent desiccation (drying) and to protect the seeds. However, marijuana grown in northern latitudes often lacks any obvious resin, yet its seeds mature and it does not desiccate. In areas where the plants produce abundant resin, it doesn't seem to be stimulated by drought; the resin usually becomes abundant late in the plant's development and it is the young plants which are the most susceptible to drought. There also does not seem to be any correlation between high resin production and high THC or CBD content. Plants often have a high cannabinoid content without being especially resinous or sticky. For these reasons it seems that the real explanations for resin production and cannabinoid content lie elsewhere.

As with virtually all other psychoactive compounds occurring in plants, the function of cannabinoids is unknown. In order to have evolved the many genes necessary for the synthesis of such complex molecules, they or their precursors probably serve an important purpose. This makes the failure to have a ready explanation for their presence all the more frustrating, especially in view of the tremendous advances in plant biochemistry. It seems likely that the cannabinoids are an important constituent of resin, which serves to protect the plant from pathogens or herbivores such as bacteria, viruses, fungi, insects and cows. It has been shown that cannabidolic and cannabigerolic acids are antibiotic to gram-positive bacteria in vitro.[3] Pathogenic attack is probably more of a problem in the wet, warm tropics (which may account for the greater resin production there). But it remains a mystery as to why THC predominates in southern latitudes and CBD in northern ones.

Humans have selected marijuana for perhaps 10,000 years for use as fiber, food and medicine. The varieties producing much resin have been carefully bred and widely distributed, and this characteristic is probably much more prominent than in ancestral hemp populations. Thus, the abundance of cannabinoids in marijuana may be due to selection by our ancestors.

## Cellular Origins of Cannabinoids

Until they are about to flower, the plants have only two types of hairs. The unicellular covering hairs (trichomes) are long and thin and end in a point (see figure 9e). These are few until the plant is one month (in warm climates) or two months (in temperate climates) old. They subsequently show a gradual increase in number and are especially common on flower-bearing branches where they form a silky down. The second type of hair (cystolith) is short, swollen at the base and set into the surrounding epidermal cells (see figure 9a). Their end is blunt and they usually contain calcium carbonate crystals. They are found mostly on the upper surface of the leaves and bracts (small specialized leaves surrounding the flowers), and sometimes on the lower surface of the branches.

When the females are about to flower, their tops become covered with multicellular glandular hairs, which appear to the eye as tiny brilliant points. When the female flower first matures, these hairs form a base of two cubical cells supported by two wedge-shaped epidermal cells and a globular head of four cells, all covered by a thin cuticle (waxy non-cellular layer). (See figure 9f). At maturity, the head may contain as many as 16 radially arranged cells, which secrete the cannabinoid containing oil that accumulates between the cells and the cuticle

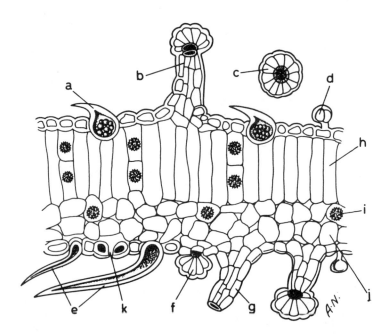

Fig. 9. Cross section of a bract from the fruiting plant: *a,* cystolith hair; *b,* large grandular hair with several cells in head and stalk; *c,* head of one of the large glandular hairs; *d,* small glandular hair with bicellular head and unicellular stalk; *e,* thick walled conical trichomes; *f,* large developing glandular hair; *g,* stalk of a large glandular hair; *h,* palisade cell; *i,* cluster crystal; *j,* parenchymal cell; *k,* stomate. (Reprinted by permission, from Joyce and Curry, *The Botany and Chemistry of Cannabis,* 1970. Drawn by D. Erasmus.)

(see figures 9b and 9c). When sufficient oil has accumulated, the cuticle may burst, releasing the oil (composed of about 50% cannabinoids), which quickly dries to form the sticky resin. Another view is that the cuticle is composed of oxidized resin.

These hairs vary in appearance: those of the bracts and axes of the female flowers develop an elongated stem and resemble a tiny mushroom, while others (especially on the lower surface of the top leaves) lack the stem and have a flat, round head with a masimum of ten cells (sessile glands). There is reason to believe that sessile glands are a distinct type and not an early stage of the stalked glands. All these cells lack chloroplasts and are color-less except for the amber oil produced in the head. Lesser amounts of cannabinoids are also produced by cells generally distributed throughout the epidermis of the plant (lactifers).[4]

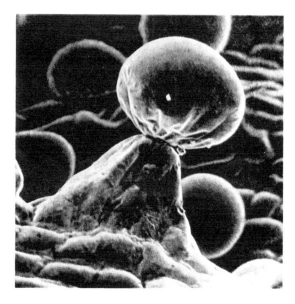

Fig. 10. Scanning electron microscope picture of the lower surface of a bracteole (seed covering) magnified 100 times. The stalked glandular hairs are seen in various stages of development. Two simple covering hairs are shown at the upper right. (Reprinted from Fairbairn, *Bulletin on Narcotics,* Vol. 24, 1972.)

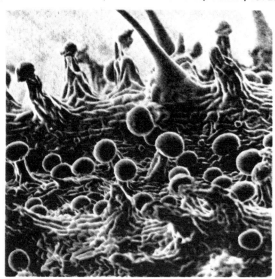

Fig. 11. Scanning electron microscope picture of a stalked glandular hair from a bracteole (seed covering) magnified 400 times. Cannabinoids are concentrated in the round head. The rectangular lumpy "bricks" are cells. (Reprinted from Fairbairn, *Bulletin on Narcotics,* Vol. 24, 1972.)

## Heredity and Environment

Regardless of seed origin, several generations in a new location will produce a plant resembling those native to the area where it is being grown. This fact has been known for centuries. In 1712, Kaempfer observed that seeds of Persian *Cannabis* failed to produce significant quantities of intoxicating resin when grown in Europe for several generations. Similarly, in the early nineteenth century, the Egyptian Viceroy, Mehemet Ali, found that the French hemp seeds he imported to provide fiber for rope were useless for that purpose. After a few growing seasons the plants became short and bushy, producing large quantities of resin. (Part of the explanation undoubtedly lies in the shorter days of Egypt.) In that same century, Christison at Edinburgh, Hope in England and Husson in Cairo observed the same phenomenon when they planted imported seeds. In a report published in 1912, pioneer marijuana researcher, J. Bouquet, described the nature of the change that can occur in only a single generation. He said that seeds from India (Guaza) and Greece (Tripolis) planted at Lyon in France produced plants about two meters talls. They were robust and bushy with many branches and large, deep-green leaves with sharply indented edges and (in the Indian variety) distinct furrows on the upper surface of the petioles (leaf stems). The petioles of the Indian variety were reddish-brown but lost their color with age. The flowers were concentrated in clusters of cymes (main and secondary branches always terminate in a single flower) and the groups of clusters were separated from one another by leaves and well-developed bracts nearly hid the flowers from view. (Bracts are modified leaves which surround and protect the flowers and, later, the seeds.) The large, vigorous flowers gave off an intense mint-like odor which was perceptible more than two meters away. At maturity, the flowering tops were covered with shiny points which were tiny reddish droplets of resin in the glandular hairs.

When the seeds from the above plants were grown the next year at Moulin-sur-Allier, the plants were little different from those commonly cultivated in France for fiber. They were only slightly bushier, and of a somewhat deeper green than the native fiber plants, but did not have the bushy flowering tops or the

furrowed, colored petioles and resin production of their ancestors. The tops were not even sticky. But seeds from the same
batch were planted the same year at Beja in Tunisia (altitude:
330 meters). The resulting plants were very similar to the first
generation Indian and Greek plants grown at Lyon, with their
bushy odiferous flowers and intense resin production.

The second generation plants at Moulin-sur-Allier may have
cross pollinated with the French fiber strains of marijuana or
may have been the result of natural selection. It is likely that if
the same 100 seeds of Indian marijuana were planted in India
and in France, we would find differences in the number of seeds
germinating. The plants which grew to adulthood would probably represent a different range of seeds in the two cases. Also,
the average genetic makeup of their seeds, even if inbred, would
probably differ, depending on the selective forces acting on the
developing seeds and pollen. The longer days of the northern
latitudes probably contribute to lengthening the internodes and
altering other characteristics of the growing plant.[5] Some experiments on the effect of day length on resin production are discussed later.

In relation to the role of a hot, dry environment in the production of the THC containing resin, observations made by
Bouquet some 40 years ago on an aberrant variety which arose
in 1935 in Tunisian crops are of great interest.

In Tunisia, it arose independently in plantations at Tabarka
and Sedjenane, located some 40 kilometers apart in the moun-
tainous region. The seeds originated as usual from the previous
year's crop, and the resulting abnormal seeds may have derived
from a very few plants of the previous year and ultimately from
a mutation occurring in a single plant.

The most striking characteristic of these plants was their
very slow maturation. Whereas the usual variety flowered and
set seed in some 14 weeks and was harvested at the beginning of
July, the new type did not set seed for 22 weeks and was collected at the middle of September. Of major importance is the
fact that its characteristics were fully heritable and plants grown
the following year in Tunis and the United States were essentially identical. There were other striking differences from normal
plants. They were slightly over a meter tall, which height, though

differing little from the usual Tunisian plants, was maintained in the U.S.A. plantings, where they were markedly shorter than the rest of the crop. The plants were branched almost to their base with an extremely bushy, compact aspect. The stems are generally larger (up to 9.5 cm in circumference at the base) and sturdier than normal with longer, stronger fibers and being more deeply ribbed or fluted, though feeling smoother to the touch. The taproot was turnip-shaped (napiform) some 12.2 cm around and 12 cm long, then tapering off to a total length of 32 cm, while the ordinary type was not napiform and generally shorter. The new variety had much more numerous adventitious roots.

The leaves were always opposite from the base of the stem to the top (always imparipinnate) while the normal variety is sometimes alternate. The leaves rarely reach 10 cm from the point of insertion on the petiole to the end of the longest median leaflet, whereas the typical leaves average 20 cm. All the leaves have seven or nine leaflets with 12 to 16 teeth on each edge compared to five, seven, nine, or 11 leaflets and 14 to 22 teeth normally. The plant has a deeper green color on upper leaf surfaces but the underside of the leaves is light green at first, becoming almost white at maturity, and thus resembling the wormwood *(Artemisia vulgaris)* leaves. The leaf veins are deeper than normal, giving the impression of regular folds in the leaflets, and being noticeably more visible on the inferior face than usual. The threadlike (filiform) stipules at the base of the petioles of the upper leaves are a deeper yellow-orange than normal. The bracts (specialized leaves surrounding the flowers) are better developed, longer and more numerous than usual, forming little tufts. The flowering tops are less numerous, more elongate or less compact than typical with 0 to 8 seeds per inflorescence compared with the normal of 40 to 60. The tops are not sticky and the minty odor is absent even when the plant is crushed between the fingers.

Microscopically, the powder from the edge of the leaflets and the bracts is gronze-green rather than yellow-green, and again lacks the characteristic odor of fresh powder. The microstructure appears normal, with double calcium oxalate crystals, and the various types of hairs—unicellular pointed, short cystolithic (containing calcium carbonate crystals), conical, swollen with blurt extremity, etc., but the clubbed, stalked (pedicellate) secretory hairs are rare, poorly developed, and for the most part devoid of the clear amber oily resin. Both male and female flowering tops give positive reactions for cannabidiol with the male reaction being weaker, as is that of the female prior to flowering.

These observations show that we cannot necessarily expect plants to be exactly like their parents in appearance or THC content, even in the first generation. In subsequent generations the difference may be even greater and the plants may soon resemble those growing wild in our area. However, if we are very careful about our pollen source, we may succeed in growing a high THC strain for many generations since, as subsequent sections show, cannabinoid production is largely a matter of genetics.

## Bonsai Marijuana

The common belief is that marijuana is an annual: it flowers and dies each year. In nature, this is probably always true, even in warm climates. (However, where it is warm year round, new plants may always be growing. There are reports that C. sativa is sometimes perennial in tropical and subtropical areas.) Nevertheless, appropriate manipulation may allow a plant to grow for years and possibly decades. Some people have kept females alive outdoors for several years by carefully trimming the flowering tops, but long-lived plants are more likely to be cultivated indoors where the environment can be carefully controlled. An individual in Los Angeles claims he has a bonsai marijuana plant in his house which has yielded an extremely potent product for more than three years. Just how much the traditional bonsai techniques, such as pruning and restricting water and nutrients, are applicable to marijuana is still unknown. This is an area where careful experimentation is necessary.

## Grafting and Cloning

Most of the interest in grafting marijuana plants arose from the

mistaken belief that hops-marijuana grafts could produce an un-
recognizable but potent plant. Even though this notion has been
proven false, grafting various *Cannabis* stocks on one another is
still of interest. For example, one plant may root well and have
a strong stem, but produce little THC, while another may be the
opposite. Or, a person might wish to have branches of four or
five different strains growing on a single plant. Each portion of
the graft will retain the cannabinoid production it had before
the graft because there is no transfer of cannabinoids. Sometimes the potency may increase somewhat after grafting because
of the stress involved, although as discussed later, this will mean
that the total yield of cannabinoids will also decrease.

Standard techniques, such as cotyledon wedge graft or
growing point wedge graft, are used on marijuana plants. The
object is to bring the vascular tissues of the scion (part grafted)
and stock (part grafted onto) into contact. The graft can then
be sealed with petroleum jelly or commercial sealing agents
and held tight with adhesive tape or rubber bands. Grafts are
most likely to be successful after the plant is well established (at
least two weeks), but before it is mature. The more active the
growth, the more likely the graft will take. One good technique
is to grow the two plants to be grafted side by side or in adjacent
containers. When they are between four and eight weeks old,
make a single diagonal cut halfway through each stem at approximately the same level, one slanted upward and one downward.
Slip the cut portions into each other and hold the joints together
with adhesive tape. After one to two weeks, cut away the un-
wanted top portion and then, a few days later, cut away the un-
wanted bottom part.

A clone is all the descendants derived asexually (vegetatively)
from a single plant. Since no sexual processes are involved, all
members of a clone are genetically identical (except for somatic
mutations). The most common way of making a clone is by
rooting cuttings. Marijuana can be cloned by cutting off a lateral
branch of a plant one to two month's old and immersing it in
water or wet sand until rooting occurs. The plant growth hor-
mone, indoleacetic acid (Rootone), can be used to stimulate
rooting. The cutting is then put in soil and grown as usual.
Lateral branching is encouraged by cutting off the growing tip

(apical meristem) at an early age, and this can be done repeatedly. Thus a single, highly potent plant can give rise to hundreds of plants. This is an obvious method for marijuana researchers who are studying the effect of environment on cannabinoid production, but so far they have (with one exception) ignored it.[6]

## Pruning Branches and Manipulating Stems

Pruning the tops of marijuana plants is the custom in Brazil. But in the Bengal area of India, the lower branches are removed when the plant is about three months old. The Nepalese supposedly trim the tips, remove the larger leaves and shake the plant from time to time; the resulting mass of twisted leaves and flowers is called *latta,* probably very similar to the *colas* of mature sinsemilla.

Splitting the base is another practice believed to increase potency. In India, farmers reportedly twist the base of the stem or the flowering tops sometime before harvest. In Mysore, they twist the stem of the two-month-old plant, then bend it horizontally and sometimes tie it in that position to encourage side branches. Still another custom, reportedly practiced by the Burmese, is to split the stem about a month before maturity and insert a piece of wood, then gather together the flowering tops and push them into a basket. The basket is inverted over the tops and left there for the final month of growth.

In Mexico, farmers insert slivers of *acote* (a type of pine) through the root of the plant below ground level when the plant is about four feet high. They claim that this prevents the formation of seeds and gives the marijuana a pine flavor, both highly unlikely.

In some parts of the Western Himalaya, plants are stripped of all, or nearly all, of their leaves in order to stimulate the formation of numerous small, leafy shoots. These shoots are supposed to be stronger than the old foliage. While no experimental work has been reported on this point, it certainly seems worth investigating.

The Tepehua of Oaxaca, Mexico produce extremely potent marijuana by growing the plants in a hostile environment and by severe pruning. They pinch off the shoot tips from the young seedlings, thus removing the apical meristem with its high concentration of auxins (plant growth hormones). This leads to the production of many lateral meristems (side shoots). The new lateral meristems are pruned once a week to produce a small, urn-shaped bush. Shoots that would ordinarily fill the interior of this "urn" are also removed. The exterior looks almost crystalline due to the heavy resin accumulation, and many plants develop a red pigmentation (cyanins). The leaves change from the ordinary palmate shape to verticillate or whorled (like the spokes of a wheel) balls of entire (smooth-edged) leaves and abortive (incomplete or immature) flowers. When the blood-like color begins to appear, two wooden splinters are inserted through the stem just above the ground at right angles to each other. At present there is no evidence that this latter practice has any effect on potency, but it is interesting that the stems are similarly bruised or impaled by various Asian farmers.

To sum up, though many peoples around the world prune marijuana plants, or split their stems, there is no scientific proof that these practices increase potency. However, as discussed later, any kind of stress tends to increase potency somewhat, though usually at the cost of decreasing the total yield.

## Potency and Color

The extreme redness of the Tepehua's plants may merely indicate the soil's potassium deficiency or may be a genetic factor which has been observed in stems and leaves elsewhere (such as Zihuatenejo purple). Red and purple colors are produced by pigments called anthocyanins. Extreme nitrogen or phosphorous deficiencies can also produce red petioles (leaf stems) or leaves. Plants are green due to the presence of large amounts of chlorophyll; the other colored pigments only show up as the plant ages and the chlorophyll degrades. The nature of the pigments producing the gold color of some Central and South American marijuana is unknown, as is their relationship to the high THC content of these varieties. Both Acapulco Gold and Colombian (or Santa Marta) Gold tend to be very potent, especially Colombian. *Punta Roja* ("red point" in Spanish) is another potent plant which comes from the Llano area of Cali Hills near Santa Marta in Colombia, and derives its name from the red color of the pistils. Marijuana can also be a blackish color, such as some grown in Africa and in Colombia ("Wacky Weed"). The dark green marijuana from the Choco area of Colombia near the Panamanian border is often nearly black.

Color is thought by some to be influenced by climate. Some persons have claimed that marijuana which matures late in cool weather tends to be a purplish color, but that the purple of the leaves, stems and/or flowers is not accompanied by increased potency.

In summary, there seems to be little relationship between potency and color, since each variety of marijuana contains plants with high, medium and low content of both THC and CBD.

## Some Growing Techniques

Fifty years ago a French pharmaceutical text described the growing of hemp for resin as follows:

> The choice of ground is important: hemp plants strike out many tap roots; the soil must therefore be light, loose and at the same time full of substance. The only preparation necessary is tilling and manuring. At least three tillings are necessary: the first takes place before the winter, the second in the spring when the weeds are beginning to grow, and the third a day or two before the sowing, about the beginning of May or June (in North Africa there are only two tillings, and sowing takes place at the end of March). The choice of fertilizers depends on the nature of the soil: horse manure, well-mixed with other fertilizers, is suitable for heavy land; cow or sheep manure is better for light soils. In Tunis a mixture of farmyard manure and superphosphates is used. The sowing is in lines 20 cm apart (in North Africa 60 cm). The arrangements in

lines makes hoeing and thinning easier. The latter operation should be effected as soon as hemp has its first two leaves; care should be taken, when superflous plants are being pulled up, not to lay bare the roots of those nearby. Once the hemp has reached a certain height, it grows rapidly. The male and female plants come up at the same time; but the former, though thinner, are taller until they have almost reached maturity . . . In Europe, harvesting takes place at the end of September, and in North Africa in July.

A successful American marijuana farmer in the southwestern U.S. described his techniques as follows. Growing on a one-acre plot with a southern exposure, he seeds with red clover after each crop of marijuana and plows the clover under before the first frost. He also plows in one ton of compost. He pulls up most of the males three different times, one week apart and hangs them upside down with a baggie over the end to collect the pollen. He pinches the tips off the female plants once at about six weeks. After about five months, some of the females start to develop male flowers. Watering is done about eight times a year, and this infrequent but deep watering results in deep roots and drought-resistant plants. The soil must be well drained and there must never be any standing water in the field. The females are harvested when they are 1/4 to 1/2 seeded, and about three dozen females are allowed to become fully seeded for next year's crop. They are then hung up for one day, the big stems removed and hung up for another week. The large tops are sold separately from the small tops and leaves.

For quantity planting, one farmer recommends a hill-drop planter which scatters five to ten seeds in a group about every three feet. The crop is later thinned to the best two plants in each group; an ordinary soy bean or corn planter with a fine seed attachment for hill-drop planting will work. As soon as the plants begin to crowd each other they should be thinned out, leaving about four feet for each female to branch out. A large, fully-grown female may yield one-half to one pound of marijuana, depending on how many seeds are present. Austrian winter peas or vetch, planted in October and turned under in March (southern U.S.), will be a good winter cover crop. Clover would also do, but it might not grow very much in winter. In the South, planting can start as early as the end of March, but at the latitude of Washington, D.C., April 15th is about the earliest possible, as marijuana will usually survive a mild frost, but not severe or repeated frosts.[7]

# Sinsemilla

Sinsemilla is a running together of the two Spanish words, meaning "without seeds." Since in nature virtually all the mature ova that the female develops will be fertilized and will set (seed), sinsemilla is necessarily produced artificially by separating the males. It is usually said that the practice of separating males was devised in ancient India to produce more potent marijuana. It may, however, have originally started in order to eliminate the troublesome seeds which are harder to separate from fresh, sticky tops, or to yield a uniform crop for fiber. When it began is unknown, but "ganja doctors," who weed out the males, have probably done so for thousands of years. The males are not difficult to weed out, since they tend to mature earlier and shed their pollen before the females on the same site are ready to be fertilized (an evolutionary advantage in that it facilitates exogamy-outbreeding). Usually, however, some male flowers will develop later, or if fertilization is delayed too long, some of the developing females will begin to produce male flowers. Consequently, one must be continually on the alert for not only male plants but also for male flowers on female plants. The tendency of females to produce male flowers varies enormously, depending on factors such as strain (seed origin), age, water, temperature and soil conditions. Remember also that a plant's ovum can be fertilized by pollen from males a block away, or from the fingers of your friends who've been rolling joints.

What happens when you take away the males is that the unfertilized female proceeds as if enraged by the frustration of her mating instincts. Instead of diverting all her energies into producing seeds and then dying, she continues to grow, producing more flowers, more leaves and more resin. She will live for up to seven more months—a frustrated but very stony old maid.

Recently a superb photoessay on sinsemilla was published. (*Sinsemilla*, And/Or Press, 1976). The author, Jim Richardson, describes the odor of the ripe blossoms as having an "electric sweetness and ethereal penetrating quality," and makes several interesting claims about potency. Richardson says that increased resin production does not necessarily mean increased potency and that the high is less clear and sweet after blooming, whether or not seed is set (i.e. whether or not sinsemilla is produced). He also talks about the possible rediscovery of an ancient Indian method of determining the sex of the plants. On the main stalk, in the second or third node below the growing tip, are a pair of spear-like leaf spurs (stipules). There is one on each side of the stalk; their tips cross if the branches are opposite at this point. Behind these spurs the first flower buds appear several weeks before the first flower clusters appear on the branches. If the plant is a female, this bud continues to grow erect and eventually develops into a characteristic female flower with two pistils. If it is a male, it soon droops over and becomes the pod-like male flower. The structure, used by the *poddar* (ganja doctor) to recognize males, turns out to be the often abortive, solitary female flowers that frequently take the place of what should be the lowest pair of male flowers. Undoubtedly the occurrence and appearance of these structures varies considerably with different strains and probably with growing conditions.

There are many methods of growing sinsemilla. One popular technique which works both indoors and outdoors in moderate climates, is to cut the plant back to one foot or so off the ground, leaving only a few leafy branches. Within a few weeks, it should begin sprouting new branches. When the new growth is securely started, remove the old branches and another crop of sinsemilla will be on its way. Hermaphrodism will be a continuing problem; watch carefully for the male flowers appearing on your female plants and pinch them off.

The time element involved in these operations will vary considerably, but the following will serve as a rough guide:

> Time after planting until weeding out first males: 8 weeks.
>
> Subsequent interval for checking male flowers: 1/2 week.
>
> Cutting back females to start another crop: 12-20 weeks.

The scientific literature does not yet contain any data on the THC or CBD content of sinsemilla. Consequently it is presently unknown, as with ordinary marijuana plants, which conditions during the later stages of growth are optimal for maximizing THC and minimizing CBD.

# Polyploidy

Polyploidy is the occurrence of some multiple of the usual chromosome number in the cells. The diploid or normal number in *Cannabis* is 20, but plants having 30 (triploid), 40 (tetraploid) or more are occasionally observed. Some species or varieties of plants are naturally occurring polyploids; i.e. they evolved from the spontaneous or accidental appearance of a polyploid seed which had some selective advantage over its diploid progenitors. Polyploids, either naturally occurring or artificaly induced, are relatively common in flowering plants. Polyploids can be produced by specific chemicals which interfere with the separation of the chromosome pairs during meiosis, but this is a rather drastic treatment which often kills the seeds or plants. Seeds which do survive frequently produce stunted, aberrant plants. But this is not always true; large, healthy, beautiful plants, such as numerous popular flowers, may result. However, even when successful, polyploid plants frequently fail to breed true; their seeds tend to revert to diploid. *Cannabis* polyploids are larger and have larger seeds (up to twice normal size) than the diploids and make take longer to mature.

This phenomenon would be of little interest here were it not for some experiments conducted by an American scientist named Warmke during World War II. Treating marijuana plants with colchicine, he obtained a number of triploid and tetraploid and tetraploid plants had about the same average activity (though individual plants varied by a factor of eight) which was about twice that of the normal diploid strains. He used 26 different plants of each variety and his data were statistically significant. Unfortunately, he worked with an acetone extract of the plants and his assay animals were small fish, making it doubtful whether his data have any relation to cannabinoid content.

Nevertheless, further investigation is necessary. It has been established that tobacco tetraploids have more nicotine than diploids, and this may prove true for the cannabinoid content of marijuana polyploids versus diploids. Again, it is to be expected that the total yield will decrease.

Warmke was also the author of the famous hops-grafting experiments, in which marijuana and hops were grafted onto one another. His data showed transfer of cannabinoids into the hops plants, but he used water fleas as his test animals and the data never had any clear relationship to cannabinoid content. Since then it's been shown that cannabinoids are produced locally and do not translocate. In any event, a recent repeat of this latter experiment using modern chemical techniques showed absolutely no transfer of cannabinoids into the hops portion of the grafts—either from the marijuana bottoms to the hops tops or from the marijuana tops to the hops bottoms. Hundreds, perhaps thousands of people, have attempted to produce more potent, or at least undetectable marijuana, on the basis of a few dead fish and water fleas. One is reminded of Mark Twain's comment: "I like science because it gives one such a wholesale return of conjecture from such a trifling investment of fact."[8]

## Potency and Cannabinoid Content

Myths about which kind of marijuana is the most potent or provides the best high are legion. One of the most important factors is individual response, and that varies considerably. Factors such as nutritional state, exercise, time of day, other drug intake, and psychological state all influence the individual's response to any drug. For example, one experiment showed that the amount of morphine required for pain relief may vary by a factor of five, depending on the time of day. Another demonstrated that an amount of amphetamine sufficient to kill most mice at one time of day will be harmless at another. Most people fail to take these factors into account and ascribe the character of the high to the contents of the marijuana. Although thousands of compounds occur in marijuana, the evidence seems to clearly indicate that virtually all of the significant physiological response is due to THC and, to a lesser extent, to CBD. CBN may be of significance if, as is rarely true, it is present at three or four times the THC concentration. CBN seems to be able to synergize with THC and increase its effect slightly. As stated before, it has also been shown that smoking CBD with THC blocks the THC high. But it is presently unclear just how much CBD is required to produce a given effect on the high. A reasonable guideline might be that CBD concentrations approaching that of THC are significant. The only other chemical variable in marijuana that seems relevant to the high is when the five carbon side chain in cannabinoids is replaced by a three carbon chain. This is the case in some marijuana from South Africa and Nepal and is true to a lesser extent in all marijuana. Three carbon THC (propyl cannabinoids) are discussed in more detail later in this book.

In examining the data in this chapter, it may prove interesting to keep in mind the following comments of a professional dope taster (The comments originally appeared in *High Times Magazine* Spring, 1975):

> *Oaxacan*—has a minty taste and is also spicy. It tingles the taste buds. The minty taste allows the throat to stay open, which means you draw more smoke into your lungs without coughing it out. It's quite airy considering its power.
>
> *Culiacan*—has that airiness but not the power.
>
> *Santa Marta Gold*—excellent intellectual high. Very creative. Very sophisticated high, but not particularly psychedelic like the best Mexican—this grass would be good for an intellectual fuck— like a mind-body communion.
>
> *Lowland Colombian*—knocks you out but it does not get you high. In other words, the narcotizing effect overwhelms the psychoactive effect.
>
> *Jamaican*—is good for fucking—it's very stimulating.
>
> *Hawaiian*—hypnotic intensity—an extremely dramatic pot. Few people could finish a joint—people would sit transfixed by the sheer power of the stuff—a high grass, lots of top end—mental.

*Wacky Weed*—a special kind of Colombian—has produced so much resin that it has stifled itself and died—that's why it's black sometimes. Wacky Weed is total. It makes you laugh, it makes everything absurd, it reduces your body to jelly—not anti-intellectual, but it's not exactly cerebral either. Sort of reminds me of quaaludes. Wacky Weed is physical stuff—I've seen people literally go into cardiac arrest.

*Thai*—to give me the momentum to get off the ground and climbing.

*Top Mexican*—astral.

Another marijuana sophisticate of my acquaintance has described the stronger types of marijuana as follows:

*Punta Roja*—from the Cali Hills of Colombia—dark green with red streaks—little taste but 8% THC—truly hallucinogenic—psychedelic rather than wirey.

*Santa Marta Gold*—6 to 8% THC—stimulating, gets you wired—not psychedelic like Punta Roja.

*Lowland Colombian (Colombian or Panama Red)*—red to red-brown—from the Llanos area and elsewhere—sleepy, narcotic.

*Colombian Green*—from the Choco area near the Panama border—very high rainfall. Nearly black—harsh on throat—about like good Mexican or Hawaiian.

*Hawaiian*—generally grown from Thai seed, so equal to the best Thai.

*Thai*—hallucinogenic at its best—definitely stronger than Colombian Gold.

*Nepalese*—harsh and not tasty, so make hash out of it.

# 3

# Variations in THC and CBD Content

## Introduction

The data summarized in this chapter have been painstakingly gathered from many scientific reports and have never before been collected together. They should provide a valuable basis for any future discussion of marijuana potency. However, certain limitations should be kept in mind. It has been established that marijuana should be air dried at least three days (or oven dried) in order to extract all the cannabinoids. But some studies have failed to do this or have not given a clear account of their procedure. Consequently, the values given are sometimes lower than they should be. Variation in sampling techniques is also a major problem. As the data show, there is dramatic variation in content of various plant parts and from plant to plant. Plants grown side by side from seeds from the same female can vary in cannabinoid content by five times or more. Other variables are season, age of plant, and even time of day. There has seldom been careful attention to all these details, and thus the data are only roughly comparable. Most studies have been done in northern latitudes (the U.S., Canada and England) where the slow maturing but high THC content southern latitude strains of marijuana either fail to mature, or, if they do mature, fail to develop the high potency and dramatic difference between males and females which they do in their native habitats. The keen-eyed will also notice that some of the marijuana widely agreed to be the world's strongest—Colombian and Hawaiian— are mostly absent from the tables, having been virtually ignored by researchers.

Much of the variation is due to fluctuation in the content of other constituents such as protein, fat and carbohydrate. Cannabinoids are secreted outside the membrane of the living cells which produce them and cease to be a part of the plant's active metabolism. Nonenzymatic dehydrogenation of THC to CBN appears to be the main reaction which occurs after the oily cannabinoids are secreted. This reaction is relatively slow, so CBN is seldom present in substantial amounts in fresh marijuana. However, in countries with extremely hot climates, such as India and Southeast Asia, the marijuana often contains significant amounts of CBN. Since cannabinoids are relatively nonvolatile (they don't evaporate) and insoluble in water, it might be expected that the *total* cannabinoid content *per plant* (including polymers) would rise slowly but continually throughout growth and level off sometime around flowering and setting seed. Virtually no data are available on this point. Researchers have failed to measure the total weight of the plant and give only the percentage of cannabinoids by weight of the dried plant. If the plant photosynthesizes rapidly and accumulates sugars, the percentage of THC will probably drop, since it synthesizes much more slowly. Therefore, drops in the concentration of THC and CBD usually mean that cannabinoids have decreased relative to the dry weight, but have not decreased in absolute amount in the plant. The one apparent exception to this is during senescence (aging and death) of the mature plant. Then, THC and CBD seem to decrease markedly without a corresponding increase in CBN. This appears to be one of the great unsolved mysteries of marijuana biology. Sometimes the explanation may be simple—such as the inclusion of the seeds in the dry weight. Another possibility is that the cannabinoids are formed into polymers which are not tested for. The formation of polymers may also account for much of the variation in CBD, THC and CBN content during growth, but there has been no research on this point.

## Age Variations

Seeds possess extremely minute quantities of cannabinoids, if any. This is difficult to determine because the bractlets which surround the seeds contain the plant's highest concentration of cannabinoids. Even careful washing with an organic solvent may leave traces on the seeds. After germination, the two seed leaves (cotyledons) appear. They also contain no cannabinoids or such small quantities that they are difficult to measure. However, within a day after the sprouting of the cotyledons the first pair of true leaves appears. These have measurable quantities of cannabinoids. A study of seeds from Thailand grown in a greenhouse found that the true leaves contained about three times as much CBD as THC and that the concentration did not change during the first three weeks of growth. The cannabinoids were being synthesized as fast as the other constituents. Another study found that Turkish plants increased their CBD content from 0.07 to 0.34% in one week and that Mexican plants increased their CBD content from 0.03 to 0.2% in three weeks. Although there were only traces of THC in the Turkish seedlings (as in the adults), Mexican seedlings rose from a mere 0.04% of THC to a respectable 0.46% at three weeks. Furthermore, at two weeks the Mexican plants showed a variation of 0.2 to 1.1% THC. The average person will get quite stoned on marijuana containing 1.1% THC. These data, coupled with those in table 2 and a reading of the literature, show that not only is the cannabinoid pattern of the mature plant already well established in the seedling, but that a two-week-old seedling may sometimes be nearly as potent as a mature plant. Table 2 shows that Mexican seeds grown in Mississippi contained only 1.6% THC at 13 weeks, but later contained two or three times this percentage. However, Turkish plants have a lower percentage CBD content at 15 weeks than they have at seven days, though the adult plants have a vastly greater total amount.

There are several practical consequences of these data for the marijuana grower. First, very young plants can be harvested and smoked; and, provided that the seeds are derived from a high THC content strain, they will be potent. Secondly, the potency of the plant does not necessarily increase continually as it gets older, but will often undergo constant variation. In one test, Mexican males went from a mediocre 1.6% THC content at 13 weeks to a whopping 5.6% at 15 weeks and then back down to a respectable 3% at 17 weeks. Bear in mind that these data are subject to sampling errors and should be taken with a grain of *Cannabis!* Also, it is possible that the THC disappears into polymers which may be psychoactive.[1]

## TABLE 2

### Variation of Cannabinoid Content with Age†

*Values in this and other tables are % dry weight, rounded off to one decimal place. Values are for dried tops rounded off to one decimal place.*

M = Male      F = Female
V = Vegetative (before flowering)      T = Trace ($<0.1\%$)

| SEED ORIGIN | GROWN IN | AGE IN WEEKS | THC M | THC V | THC F | CBD M | CBD V | CBD F |
|---|---|---|---|---|---|---|---|---|
| Turkey | Mississippi | 8 | T | | T | 0.1 | | 0.2 |
| | | 11 | T | | T | 0.2 | | 0.2 |
| | | 15 | T | | T | 0.3 | | 0.3 |
| | | 18 | T | | T | 0.5 | | 0.9 |
| | | 19 | — | | 0.1 | — | | 1.0 |
| Mexico | Mississippi | 5 | | 0.5 | | | 0.1 | |
| | | 7 | | 0.7 | | | 0.1 | |
| | | 9 | | 2.5 | | | 0.2 | |
| | | 11 | | 1.7 | | | 0.1 | |
| | | 13 | 1.6 | | 1.6 | 0.6 | | 0.6 |
| | | 15 | 5.6 | | 3.3 | 0.6 | | 0.2 |
| | | 17 | 3.0 | | 2.9 | 0.1 | | 0.2 |
| | | 19 | 3.0 | | 4.0 | 0.2 | | 0.4 |
| Japan | Japan | 2 | | 0.1 | | | 0.1 | |
| | | 4 | | 0.2 | | | 0.3 | |
| | | 8 | 0.4 | | 0.3 | 0.1 | | 0.2 |
| | | 12 | 0.8 | | 0.1 | 0.2 | | T |
| | | 16 | 0.4 | | 0.9 | 0.1 | | T |
| | | 20 | — | | 0.7 | — | | 0.2 |
| Japan | Japan | 18 | | | 2.7* | | | |
| | | 21 | | | 5.8 | | | |
| | | 22 | | | 6.6 | | | |
| | | 23 | | | 8.4 | | | |

| SEED ORIGIN | GROWN IN | AGE IN WEEKS | THC | | | CBD | | |
|---|---|---|---|---|---|---|---|---|
| | | | M | V | F | M | V | F |
| Japan | Japan | 24 | | | 9.4 | | | |
| | | 27 | | | 10.9 | | | |

*Values for bractlets (ages approximate)
†See text for discussion of sampling techniques

SOURCE: P.S. Fetterman et al., "Mississippi Grown *Cannabis sativa* L.," *Journal of Pharmaceutical Science* 60 (1971): 1246; C.E. Turner et al., "Constituents of *Cannabis sativa* L. X.," *Acta Pharmaceutica Jugoslavica* 25 (1975): 7; H. Kaneshima et al., "Studies on *Cannabis* in Hokkaido, Part 5," *Hokkaidoritsu Eisei Kenkyushoho* 23 (1973): 1.

# Cannabinoid Phenotypes

There are two basic types of marijuana plants: those cultivated for their fiber content and those cultivated for their drug content. The fiber type is generally grown in temperate climates and is useful for making cloth, rope and paper. It yields little or no drug. The drug type is generally grown in warmer, drier countries and is less useful for fiber. The fiber type has usually been called *Cannabis sativa*, and the drug type *Cannabis indica*. Distinct groups within a species which differ in their form, chemical content and behavior are known as phenotypes (literally, visible types). Genotype, on the other hand, refers to the genes or hereditary makeup of an organism. The phenotypic differences which exist in various strains or stocks of marijuana with respect to their content are the result of different genes interacting with environmental variables. In order to enhance marijuana potency, we can manipulate growth conditions as well as exercise considerable care in the selection of seeds.

In the last century, breeding programs have led to the development of several hundred distinct varieties. Virtually all of these have been selected for the fiber content of their stems or the oil content of their seeds, with little emphasis on their drug content. However, recently there has been considerable research on determining the relative amounts of cannabinoids in various types of marijuana and delineating possible phenotypes with respect to their THC and CBD content. The results so far indicate that plants from temperate climates tend to have a high CBD and low THC content, while those from warm southern areas tend to have low CBD and high THC content. Four phenotypes have been described, and a fifth is proposed here:

**Type I**    High THC and low CBD in both males and females; matures slowly; is usually native to areas below latitude 30° North (which runs through Morocco, Iran, N. India, S. China, N. Mexico and Florida).

**Type II**   Moderate levels of CBD and THC with higher CBD, and females having more of both; usually matures rapidly; native to regions north of latitude 30° North.

**Type III**  Moderate to high levels of CBD with low levels of THC, and females having more of both; usually matures rapidly; native to regions north of latitude 30° North.

**Type IV**   High THC and low CBD in both males and females; matures slowly; native to northeastern Asia (Japan, Korea, N. China). Has small quantities of cannabigerol monomethyl ether (an inactive cannabinoid). Plants often very tall.

**Type V**    High THC and very low CBD in both males and females; matures slowly; native to Indonesia, Southern Africa, and Nepal. Up to 80% of the THC is actually THCV (tetrahydrocannivarin) with a propyl side chain replacing the amyl side chain of THC.

These phenotypes appear to have a solid genetic basis since, as the data in the tables will show, seeds from these types produce essentially the same kind of marijuana no matter where they are grown. The slow maturing, high THC types are adapted for conditions near the equator where longer growing seasons allow them to develop fully. A great deal of variation exists and there is much overlap, particularly between types II and III. It is possible that the phenotypes were much more distinct in the past when transport of seeds from every area of the world was limited. Hybrids between the types seem to be completely fertile and to contain cannabinoids approximately intermediate between those of the parents, though the offspring may often deviate to either the high or low THC parent. It would be extreme-

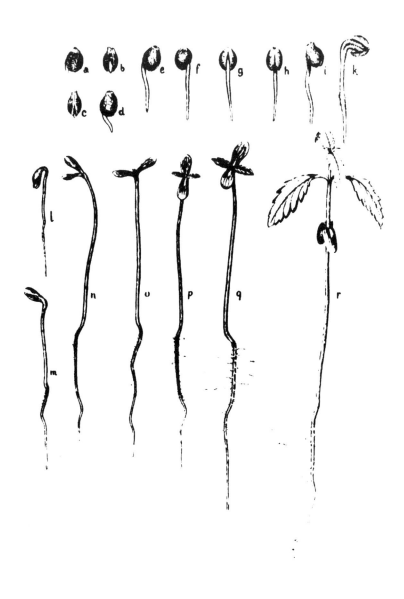

Fig. 12. Germination of a marijuana seed: *a-c,* three views after 24 hours of germination; *d,* after 48 hours; *e,* after three days; *f-i,* after four days; *k,* after five days; *l-q,* after six to ten days; *r,* after two to four weeks. *A-k* are twice their natural size; *l-r* are natural size. (Reprinted from H. Walter, *Lebengeschichte der Blutenpflanzen Mitteleuropas,* vol. 2, 1935.)

ly interesting to follow the THC content of a high THC southern strain raised in the north through several inbred generations to determine whether, if it is protected against cross fertilization by the native low THC strains, it can maintain its high THC output. There is, however, the continual problem of natural selection. All marijuana seeds, including those of inbred strains, vary considerably. Furthermore, the slower developing plants will have little, if any, mature seeds when it is time to harvest in the northern climates. Consequently, they will be under represented (if at all) in the second generation. Sensitivity to the other factors which influence the percentage of seeds that germinate and rate of development of the seeds also varies in each strain of marijuana. This means that even if the plants are inbred and grown under carefully controlled conditions, the average genetic makeup of the population will probably change for each generation. There seems to be only one well-controlled experiment on this point. High THC South African seeds were grown in temperate areas by some half-dozen growers and produced so little CBD that it was virtually undetectable, as well as significant amounts of propyl cannabinoids. A careful study in a phytotron (growth chamber) over three generations at a high and a low temperature showed no CBD and little variation in cannabinoid content. Content was always higher at lower temperatures. However, by the third generation, natural selection had eliminated the plants which had large amounts of propyl cannabinoids.

Some data exist for second or third generations from other studies such as the one at the University of Mississippi previously referred to. However, in those studies there was little control over pollination, which means that the second generation Mexican seeds could be a cross between Mexican and Nepalese—or any other males that happened to mature at the right time, within a hundred yards or so.[2]

# Relative Potency of Male and Female Plants

The first observations about the differences in potency of the male and female marijuana plants were probably made thousands of years ago. The ancient Indian practice of separating males

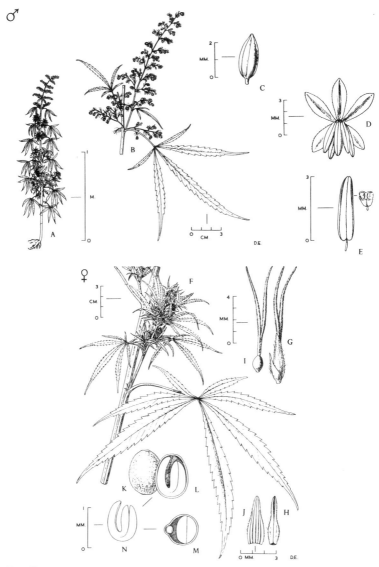

Fig. 13. Anatomy of male and female *Cannabis: A,* mature male plant; *B,* mature male flowering branch; *C,* immature closed male flower; *D,* mature open male flower with 5 sepals surrounding 5 anthers; *E,* single anther and cross section of anther containing pollen; *F,* female flowering branch containing many flowers and bracts; *G,* female flower with 2 projecting stigmas; *H,* bractlet removed from around female flower; *I,* female flower with bractlet removed showing ovary and 2 stigmas; *J,* inside of bractlet; *K,* outside of seed; *L,* seed in longitudinal section showing embryo; *M,* seed in cross section; *N,* embryo removed from seed showing root and cotyledon. (Reprinted, by permission, from Joyce and Curry, *The Botany and Chemistry of Cannabis,* 1970. Drawn by D. Erasmus.)

from females is often cited as evidence of this, but in fact this is done in order to prevent or diminish fertilization of the females. The lesser potency of the males need not have anything to do with the practice. Males are sometimes culled out in fiber-producing countries because they mature earlier and die, and because they are a different height.

Actually, the male plants are the victim of bad press. Males often equal or exceed females in cannabinoid content, especially in the high THC strains (see table 3). In fact, usually the females are only more potent during the terminal stages of development when the males are dying and the females are in full flower or are setting seed (see table 2). If the males could be prevented from flowering by pruning, flower removal or chemicals, they might continue to develop potency on a par with females. Males, however, are much more difficult to manipulate than females. For example, their flowering is not triggered by decreasing day length as the females' generally is, but is relatively fixed and inherent in each strain. Pinching the flowers before they open is difficult because males tend to produce flowers all over the plant, especially when they are frustrated by bothersome human fingers.

In the University of Mississippi experiments, the male and female Mexican plants had identical cannabinoid contents when first measured at 13 weeks, and were still about equal even at 17 weeks (see table 2). Note that many of the males die by 17 weeks and that the later measurements refer to the more slowly developing males. The table also shows that high CBD, low THC strains behave similarly to the high THC strains.

The cannabinoid content of males and females in high THC strains tends to be about the same, with the males sometimes exceeding the females. But, in the intermediate and low THC strains, the males tend to have a noticeably lower content. These data are not totally reliable, however, because the sampling techniques, growth conditions and degree of maturity varied drastically. Erratic sampling may also explain the aberrant data presented at the end of table 3. In a high THC strain from Afghanistan, the female has the expected small amount of CBD, but the male has a whopping 4.6%; whereas in another Afghani strain the males and females have about equal amounts of CBD, but the male has nearly five times as much THC. In one Turkish strain the males have about four times as much of both CBD and THC. There are strains from India, Peru, Thailand and Czechoslovakia in which the male is high in CBD and the female high in THC. One strain from Iran has both sexes low in THC but the male high in CBD, while one Manchurian and one Thai strain have both sexes high in THC, but only the female high in CBD. Finally, in one Russian strain the male is high in THC and the female high in CBD. Some of the seeds may have been hybrids, or mixtures of different batches of seeds. Nevertheless, these data alert us to the possibility that there are strains with drastic differences between males and females.

## TABLE 3

### Comparison of Male and Female Plants

*Each set of values represents a different seed stock.*
*Figures rounded off to one decimal place.*
*THC and CBD are given in % dry weight of manicured*
*mature flowering tops unless otherwise noted.*

M = Male      F = Female      T = Trace (< 0.1%)

### High THC Strains (Female ≥ 0.5%)

| SEED ORIGIN | GROWN IN | CONDITION | SEX | THC | CBD |
|---|---|---|---|---|---|
| Argentina | Argentina | Flowering | F | 0.5 | 0.7 |
|  |  |  | M | 0.5 | 0.5 |
| Chile | Canada | Immature | F | 0.8 | 0.1 |
|  |  |  | M | 0.1 | 0.2 |
| Gambia | Canada | Immature | F | 1.0 | 0.1 |
|  |  |  | M | 0.7 | 0.1 |
| India | Mississippi | Flowering | F | 1.3 | 0.9 |
|  |  |  | M | 0.8 | 2.1 |
| Japan | Canada | Immature | F | 1.4 | 0.3 |
|  |  |  | M | 0.5 | 0.1 |
|  |  | Immature | F | 0.6 | 0.3 |
|  |  |  | M | 0.5 | 0.3 |

| SEED ORIGIN | GROWN IN | CONDITION | SEX | THC | CBD |
|---|---|---|---|---|---|
| Japan | Japan | Flowering | F | 4.8 | — |
| | | Bracts | M | 2.6 | — |
| | | Flowering | F | 1.9 | — |
| | | Leaves | M | 0.6 | — |
| | | Flowering | F | 1.2 | 0.2 |
| | | | M | 1.4 | 0.2 |
| | | Flowering | F | 0.9 | T |
| | | | M | 0.4 | T |
| | | Flowering | F | 2.1 | — |
| | | | M | 0.4 | — |
| Korea | Mississippi | Flowering | F | 0.9 | 0.1 |
| | | | M | 1.2 | 0.2 |
| Mexico | Mississippi | Flowering | F | 1.8 | T |
| | | | M | 1.7 | 0.1 |
| | | Flowering | F | 4.0 | 0.4 |
| | | | M | 3.0 | 0.2 |
| Mexico | Mississippi | Flowering | F | 1.0 | 0.1 |
| | | | M | 1.2 | 0.3 |
| | | Flowering | F | 3.7 | 0.4 |
| | | | M | 3.7 | 0.9 |
| Netherlands | Canada | Flowering | F | 1.4 | 0.2 |
| | | | M | 0.3 | 0.1 |
| Poland | Canada | Flowering | F | 1.1 | 0.7 |
| | | | M | T | 0.4 |
| South Africa | Denmark | Immature | F | 1.7 | T |
| | | | M | 0.3 | T |
| South Africa | Mississippi | Flowering | F | 2.0 | 0.6 |
| | | | M | 2.9 | 0.1 |
| Sweden | Canada | Flowering | F | 0.9 | 0.6 |
| | | | M | 0.1 | 0.6 |

| SEED ORIGIN | GROWN IN | CONDITION | SEX | THC | CBD |
|---|---|---|---|---|---|
| Thailand | Mississippi | Flowering | F | 2.5 | 0.4 |
| - | | | M | 2.4 | 0.2 |
| Vietnam | Mississippi | Flowering | F | — | — |
| | | | M | 3.2 | 0.5 |

## Intermediate Strains (F≥0.6% THC; F ≥ 0.8% CBD)

| SEED ORIGIN | GROWN IN | CONDITION | SEX | THC | CBD |
|---|---|---|---|---|---|
| Czechoslovakia | Canada | Flowering | F | 0.7 | 0.8 |
| | | | M | 0.1 | 0.3 |
| England | Canada | Flowering | F | 0.6 | 1.5 |
| | | | M | 0.1 | 0.4 |
| Ethiopia | Mississippi | Flowering | F | — | — |
| | | | M | 1.3 | 3.1 |
| Germany | Canada | Flowering | F | 0.6 | 1.4 |
| | | | M | 0.1 | 0.2 |
| India | Canada | Flowering | F | 0.6 | 0.7 |
| | | | M | 0.3 | 0.3 |
| Morocco | Mississippi | Flowering | F | 0.7 | 0.7 |
| | | | M | 0.2 | 0.4 |
| Poland | Canada | Flowering | F | 1.1 | 0.7 |
| | | | M | T | 0.4 |
| Rumania | Canada | Flowering | F | 0.6 | 1.3 |
| | | | M | T | 0.2 |
| Sweden | Canada | Flowering | F | 0.9 | 0.6 |
| | | | M | 0.1 | 0.6 |
| Thailand | Mississippi | Flowering | F | 1.4 | 2.4 |
| | | | M | 1.9 | 2.2 |
| Turkey | Mississippi | Flowering | F | 2.8 | 1.9 |
| | | | M | — | — |
| Turkey | Canada | Flowering | F | 1.3 | 1.3 |
| | | | M | 0.2 | 0.4 |

| SEED ORIGIN | GROWN IN | CONDITION | SEX | THC | CBD |
|---|---|---|---|---|---|
| USSR | Canada | Flowering | F | 0.7 | 1.3 |
|  |  |  | M | 0.2 | 0.2 |
| Yugoslavia | Canada | Flowering | F | 0.6 | 1.0 |
|  |  |  | M | T | 0.2 |

## High CBD Low THC Strains (F ≤ 0.5% THC; F ≥ 0.6% CBD)

| SEED ORIGIN | GROWN IN | CONDITION | SEX | THC | CBD |
|---|---|---|---|---|---|
| Canada | Canada | Flowering | F | 0.2 | 1.2 |
|  |  |  | M | 0.4 | 0.2 |
|  |  | Flowering | F | 0.1 | 1.7 |
|  |  |  | M | T | 0.2 |
|  |  | Flowering | F | T | 2.0 |
|  |  |  | M | T | 0.4 |
| Czechoslovakia | Canada | Flowering | F | 0.5 | 3.2 |
|  |  |  | M | 0.1 | 0.5 |
|  |  | Flowering | F | 0.2 | 1.5 |
|  |  |  | M | T | 0.5 |
|  |  | Flowering | F | T | 1.2 |
|  |  |  | M | T | 0.2 |
| England | Canada | Flowering | F | 0.1 | 2.0 |
|  |  |  | M | T | 0.3 |
|  |  | Flowering | F | 0.2 | 1.1 |
|  |  |  | M | T | 0.3 |
| France | Canada | Flowering | F | 0.1 | 2.8 |
|  |  |  | M | T | 0.3 |
|  |  | Flowering | F | T | 1.9 |
|  |  |  | M | 0.1 | 0.9 |
| France | Canada | Flowering | F | 0.4 | 1.8 |
|  |  |  | M | T | 0.4 |
| Germany | Canada | Flowering | F | 0.5 | 1.3 |
|  |  |  | M | 0.1 | 0.2 |

| SEED ORIGIN | GROWN IN | CONDITION | SEX | THC | CBD |
|---|---|---|---|---|---|
| Germany | Canada | Flowering | F | 0.4 | 0.8 |
|  |  |  | M | T | 0.5 |
|  |  | Flowering | F | 0.1 | 2.7 |
|  |  |  | M | T | 0.6 |
| Hungary | Canada | Flowering | F | 0.5 | 1.5 |
|  |  |  | M | T | 0.1 |
|  |  | Flowering | F | T | 1.6 |
|  |  |  | M | T | 0.1 |
| India | Canada | Flowering | F | 0.3 | 1.2 |
|  |  |  | M | 0.2 | 0.7 |
| Ireland | Canada | Flowering | F | 0.1 | 0.8 |
|  |  |  | M | T | 0.2 |
| Israel | Canada | Flowering | F | 0.2 | 1.0 |
|  |  |  | M | 0.2 | 0.2 |
|  |  | Flowering | F | 0.5 | 0.7 |
|  |  |  | M | 0.1 | 0.4 |
| Italy | Canada | Flowering | F | 0.1 | 1.9 |
|  |  |  | M | T | 0.2 |
|  |  | Flowering | F | T | 2.8 |
|  |  |  | M | T | 0.3 |
|  |  | Flowering | F | 0.5 | 0.6 |
|  |  |  | M | T | 0.3 |
| Lebanon | Lebanon | Flowering | F | T | 2.8 |
|  |  |  | M | 0.2 | 1.6 |
|  |  | Flowering | F | 0.4 | 0.3 |
|  |  |  | M | 0.6 | 0.7 |
| Morocco | Mississippi | Flowering | F | 0.1 | 1.6 |
|  |  |  | M | 0.4 | 1.0 |
| Netherlands | Canada | Flowering | F | 0.1 | 1.3 |
|  |  |  | M | 0.2 | 0.2 |

| SEED ORIGIN | GROWN IN | CONDITION | SEX | THC | CBD |
|---|---|---|---|---|---|
| Netherlands | Canada | Flowering | F | 0.4 | 2.1 |
| | | | M | T | 0.2 |
| Poland | Canada | Flowering | F | 0.4 | 0.7 |
| | | | M | T | 0.3 |
| | | Flowering | F | 0.2 | 1.7 |
| | | | M | T | 0.3 |
| Portugal | Canada | Flowering | F | 0.2 | 1.3 |
| | | | M | T | 0.4 |
| Rumania | Canada | Flowering | F | 0.1 | 1.9 |
| | | | M | T | 0.1 |
| Spain | Canada | Flowering | F | 0.4 | 2.7 |
| | | | M | T | 0.4 |
| Sweden | Canada | Flowering | F | 0.3 | 1.4 |
| | | | M | T | 0.4 |
| | | Flowering | F | 0.4 | 2.2 |
| | | | M | T | 0.4 |
| Turkey | Canada | Flowering | F | T | 0.5 |
| | | | M | T | 0.4 |
| | | Flowering | F | 0.1 | 0.8 |
| | | | M | T | 0.4 |
| USA (Illinois) | Canada | Flowering | F | 0.1 | 0.4 |
| | | | M | 0.1 | 0.3 |
| USA (Kansas) | Kansas | Flowering | F | T | 0.9 |
| | | | M | T | 0.3 |
| USA (Iowa) | Canada | Flowering | F | 0.1 | 1.0 |
| | | | M | 0.1 | 0.6 |
| USA (Minnesota) | Canada | Flowering | F | 0.1 | 1.6 |
| | | | M | T | 0.2 |
| USSR | Canada | Flowering | F | T | 0.6 |
| | | | M | T | 0.3 |

| SEED ORIGIN | GROWN IN | CONDITION | SEX | THC | CBD |
|---|---|---|---|---|---|
| USSR | Canada | Flowering | F | 0.1 | 3.4 |
| | | | M | T | 0.4 |
| | | Flowering | F | 0.4 | 1.6 |
| | | | M | 0.1 | 0.2 |
| Yugoslavia | Canada | Flowering | F | 0.4 | 1.4 |
| | | | M | 0.1 | 0.1 |
| | | Flowering | F | 0.2 | 0.2 |
| | | | M | 0.1 | 0.5 |

## Aberrant Data

| SEED ORIGIN | GROWN IN | CONDITION | SEX | THC | CBD |
|---|---|---|---|---|---|
| Afghanistan | Mississippi | Flowering | F | 2.1 | 0.2 |
| | | | M | 2.6 | 4.6 |
| | | Flowering | F | 0.6 | 1.3 |
| | | | M | 2.7 | 1.9 |
| Czechoslovakia | Mississippi | Flowering | F | 1.0 | 0.3 |
| | | | M | 0.1 | 1.3 |
| India | Mississippi | Flowering | F | 2.7 | T |
| | | | M | 0.1 | 2.2 |
| Iran | Mississippi | Flowering | F | 0.3 | 0.1 |
| | | | M | 0.2 | 1.6 |
| Manchuria | Mississippi | Flowering | F | 2.0 | 1.9 |
| | | | M | 1.5 | T |
| Pakistan | Mississippi | Flowering | F | 0.7 | 1.3 |
| | | | M | 1.4 | 1.2 |
| Peru | Mississippi | Flowering | F | 2.1 | T |
| | | | M | T | 0.5 |
| Russia | Mississippi | Flowering | F | 0.1 | 1.8 |
| | | | M | 1.1 | T |

| SEED ORIGIN | GROWN IN | CONDITION | SEX | THC | CBD |
|-------------|----------|-----------|-----|-----|-----|
| Thailand | Mississippi | Flowering | F | 2.9 | T |
|  |  |  | M | 0.9 | 2.3 |
|  |  | Flowering | F | 1.6 | 1.2 |
|  |  |  | M | 1.7 | T |
| Turkey | Mississippi | Flowering | F | 0.4 | 0.8 |
|  |  |  | M | 1.6 | 2.8 |

SOURCE: P.S. Fetterman et al., "Mississippi Grown *Cannabis sativa* L.," *Journal of Pharmaceutical Science* 60 (1971): 1246; J.H. Holley et al., "Constituents of *Cannabis sativa* L. XI," *Journal of Pharmaceutical Science* 64 (1975): 892; J.W. Fairbairn and J.A. Liebmann, "The Cannabinoid Content of *Cannabis sativa* L. Grown in England," *Journal of Pharmacy and Pharmacology* 26 (1974): 413; A. Ohlsson et al., "Constituents of Male and Female *Cannabis sativa*," *Bulletin on Narcotics* 23 (1971): 29; E. Small and H. Beckstead, "Common Cannabinoid Phenotypes in 350 Stocks of *Cannabis*," *Lloydia* 36 (1973): 144.

## Monoecious Strains

Marijuana plants are often hermaphrodites. Male flowers will frequently sprout forth on female plants, particularly under adverse conditions, and strains are known in which nearly every plant contains both sexes. Such monoecious strains have been specially developed for fiber production because they yield a uniform crop which matures simultaneously (the males of dioe-. cious strains usually die about one month earlier than females). The monoecious strains contain little THC; even hermaphrodites from mostly dioecious strains are of the low THC, high CBD variety (see tables 4 and 5). It seems that it should be possible to develop high THC monoecious strains as well. One monoecious female Thai plant had 2.5% THC and 0.3% CBD, while a male of the same strain had 2.1 and 0.4%, respectively. It should also be kept in mind that the designation of a plant as monoecious is often rather arbitrary, since many individuals have few male flowers. Hemp breeders have also developed seeds which will yield nearly 100% females (produced by crossing two highly inbred strains).

## Cannabinoid Content of Hashish

When we examine the cannabinoid content of hashish, we reach some very interesting conclusions. First, the actual content of

## TABLE 4

### Cannabinoid Content of Monoecious Strains
*See table 2 for details*

| SEED ORIGIN | GROWN IN | CONDITION | THC | CBD |
|---|---|---|---|---|
| Bulgaria | Canada | Flowering | T | 0.2 |
| | | Flowering | 0.2 | 0.3 |
| | | Flowering | T | 0.3 |
| France | Canada | Flowering | T | 1.0 |
| | | Flowering | T | 0.5 |
| | | Flowering | T | 0.2 |
| Germany | Canada | Flowering | 0.1 | 0.7 |
| | | Flowering | 0.1 | 0.1 |
| | | Flowering | T | 0.5 |
| Poland | Canada | Flowering | T | 0.1 |
| | | Flowering | T | 0.3 |
| | | Flowering | T | 0.6 |
| USSR | Canada | Flowering | T | 0.4 |
| | | Flowering | 0.1 | 0.5 |
| Yugoslavia | Canada | Flowering | T | 0.5 |
| | | Flowering | 0.1 | 0.4 |
| USA* | Canada | Flowering | 0.1 | 0.7 |
| | | Flowering | T | 1.3 |
| | | Flowering | 0.3 | 0.4 |
| | | Flowering | 0.2 | 0.5 |

*Double backcross of Turkish to German Monoecious

SOURCE: E. Small and H. Beckstead, "Common Cannabinoid Phenotypes in 350 Stocks of *Cannabis*," *Lloydia* 36 (1973): 144.

THC is extremely low considering the price. The highest amount given in table 6 (11.5%) is not even twice the amount present in good quality marijuana from Africa, India, Mexico or Colombia, and it is accompanied by so much CBD that the high will be significantly diminished. In fact, there is almost always more CBD than THC in hashish, sometimes as much as ten times more. This validates the frequent observation that hash promises much more than it delivers. An ounce of average quality hash from the Near East, costing $100, would provide about 1.4 g of THC along with a sizeable quantity of the inhibitory CBD. The same $100 would buy two ounces of marijuana which would contain an almost equal amount of THC with very little CBD. Remember, though, that the CBD may contribute to the pleasantness of the hash high.

## TABLE 5

**Comparison of Monoecious Plants with Females of Same Strain**
*See table 2 for details*
F = Female　　　B = Monoecious

| SEED ORIGIN | GROWN IN | CONDITION | SEX | THC | CBD |
|---|---|---|---|---|---|
| France | Canada | Flowering | F | 0.2 | 0.9 |
|  |  |  | B | 0.1 | 0.3 |
|  |  | Flowering | F | T | 0.9 |
|  |  |  | B | T | 1.0 |
|  |  | Flowering | F | 0.1 | 1.2 |
|  |  |  | B | 0.1 | 0.2 |
|  |  | Flowering | F | 0.1 | 0.3 |
|  |  |  | B | T | 0.8 |
| Germany | Canada | Flowering | F | 0.1 | 1.2 |
|  |  |  | B | T | 0.3 |
|  |  | Flowering | F | T | 0.5 |
|  |  |  | B | 0.1 | 0.1 |
| Poland | Canada | Flowering | F | 0.2 | 0.4 |
|  |  |  | B | T | 0.1 |
|  |  | Flowering | F | T | 0.9 |
|  |  |  | B | T | 0.3 |

SOURCE: E. Small and H. Beckstead, "Common Cannabinoid Phenotypes in 350 Stocks of *Cannabis*," *Lloydia* 36 (1973): 144.

The extremely high CBD content of hashish is puzzling. It is be expected in hashish from areas which have high CBD marijuana, but it is at first quite surprising to find it in samples from Afghanistan, Nepal and Morocco, which typically produce high THC, low CBD type plants. Part of the answer probably can be found in the adulteration with material from young plants and poor quality plants. It is also probable that the origins of some of the samples are incorrectly identified. Furthermore, the published data on marijuana is biased toward high THC strains, since many of the seeds used were seized in illicit traffic.

However, when all the available data are examined (see tables), it is clear that plants with high CBD and low to moderate THC are common in the countries where hashish originates and which preponderate in its manufacture. It may be that low-quality marijuana is earmarked for hashish. The more knowledgeable farmers in Mexico, Colombia and Southeast Asia have already begun hashish manufacture, and their product should be very potent since it is being made from high THC, low CBD plants. The maximum content will not usually exceed that of the flowering tops, except when made from hand-rubbed resin, or the top quality made by the sifting method.

Some of the older accounts of hashish preparation refer to the inclusion of pollen. This is probably a mistake; they are undoubtedly referring to the powdery fragments of the female tops. A mature crop of females will include few males, and microscopic analysis of hashish has rarely revealed more than traces of pollen. Pollen had been thought to be quite potent until recent data proved otherwise (see table 7).

## TABLE 6

### Cannabinoid Content of Hashish

| SOURCE | COLOR | % OF TOTAL WEIGHT | |
| --- | --- | --- | --- |
| | | THC | CBD |
| Afghanistan | Dark Brown | 1.7 | — |
| Afghanistan | Dark Brown | 6.5 | — |
| Lebanon | — | 1.4 | 1.4 |

| SOURCE | COLOR | % OF TOTAL WEIGHT THC | CBD |
|---|---|---|---|
| Greece | — | 2.1 | 9.8 |
| — | — | 0.7 | 0.3 |
| — | — | 0.6 | 2.3 |
| — | — | 11.5 | 15.8 |
| — | — | 4.5 | 4.7 |
| — | — | 1.7 | 1.0 |
| Pakistan | Dark Brown | 2.3 | — |
| Pakistan | Dark Brown | 8.7 | 6.3 |
| Pakistan | Dark Brown | 6.6 | — |
| Lebanon | Light Brown | 1.9 | — |
| Morocco | Light Brown | 2.0 | — |
| Nepal | Dark Brown | 1.5 | 15.1 |
| — | Dark Brown | 1.4 | — |
| — | Dark Brown | 7.1 | — |
| — | Dark Brown | 2.4 | — |
| — | Dark Brown | 3.7 | 10.6 |
| — | Dark Brown | 10.9 | — |
| — | Dark Brown | 3.9 | — |
| — | Light Brown | 4.6 | 8.8 |
| — | Light Brown | 10.5 | — |
| — | Light Brown | 0.1 | — |

## TABLE 6A

### Cannabinoid Content of Hashish

*Individual cannabinoids as percent of total cannabinoids in sample*

CBDV = Cannabidivarin      THCV = Tetrahydrocannabivarin

| SOURCE | NO. OF SAMPLES | THC | CBD | THCV | CBDV |
|---|---|---|---|---|---|
| Lebanon | 7 | 25-36 | 59-66 | — | — |
| Pakistan | 19 | 15-53 | 39-57 | — | — |

| SOURCE | NO. OF SAMPLES | THC | CBD | THCV | CBDV |
|---|---|---|---|---|---|
| Afghanistan | 5 | 42-61 | 35-45 | – | – |
| Nepal | 3 | 3-12 | 36-41 | 2-6 | 9-12 |
| Morocco | 5 | 49-60 | 31-40 | – | – |

SOURCE: K.H. Davis et al., "The Preparation and Analysis of Enriched and Pure Cannabinoids from Marihuana and Hashish," *Lloydia* 33 (1970): 453; F. Merkus, "Cannabivarin and Tetrahydrocannabivarin, Two Constituents of Hashish," *Nature* 232 (1971): 579; P.S. Fetterman et al., "Mississippi Grown *Cannabis sativa* L.," *Journal of Pharmaceutical Science* 60 (1971): 1246; P. Chambon et al., "Problemes Poses Par la Culture Locale du Chanvre et Dosage des Chanvre," *Bulletin des Traveaux de la Societe de Pharmacie de Lyon* 16 (1972): 46.

## Cannabinoid Content of Various Plant Parts

Anyone who has tried smoking the bottom leaves of even a mature plant knows that it can be a very unrewarding experience. However, if just the very tips of the flowering tops are harvested, even the most mediocre homegrown can yield potent marijuana. The bractlets (the tiny modified leaves surrounding the seeds) have the highest cannabinoid content, averaging about twice that of the bracts (see table 7). The bracts are the modified leaves which, with the flowers, form clumps at the ends of the flowering branches. Flowers tend to have more cannabinoids than bracts, though as the table shows, this may vary from nearly equal to three times as much for a particular strain. The cannabinoid content of the leaves decreases gradually from the top to the bottom of the plant. Smaller stems have even less, seldom exceeding 0.1% THC or CBD. Larger stems have almost none, and seeds and roots have little, if any.

The data on South African marijuana grown in England show that while the top leaves always have a higher content than the bottom or middle ones, the ratios vary considerably. The top leaves can have between two to ten times more THC than the bottom leaves on the same plant. The ratios of top, middle and bottom for three plants were 8, 4, 1; 1.7, 1.4, 1; and 3, 2, 1. A general principle that helps to make sense of all the data on cannabinoid content is that as the cannabinoid concentration increases, the differences become more pronounced. For example, the differences between high and low content of THC in two plants may be very obvious in the flowering tops, but undetectable in the bottom stems. Also, when the contents are low enough, one may find a reversal of the usual pattern and observe middle leaves with higher content than top leaves (such as the female Turkish plants grown in Sweden), or bottom leaves and stem having equal amounts.

The ratio of the cannabinoid content of the various parts of the plant in males versus females or of one strain versus another also varies widely and often erratically. For example, in the flowering tops of one Lebanese strain, the females had five times more THC than the males, but in the top leaves the males had twice the THC of the females. While top leaves of the U.S.S.R. and Turkish females had equal amounts of CBD, the Turkish females had equal amounts of CBD, the Turkish middle leaves had seven times more than the Russian ones (see table 7). Similarly, the ratio of CBD to THC in the various parts may vary greatly. In accordance with the general principle stated above, this ratio tends to be higher in parts where the cannabinoids are concentrated and in younger parts (since CBD is the probable precursor of THC). In one Lebanese strain, the CBD content in the female flowers was 70 times the THC, while in the top leaves it was 35 times, and in the bottom leaves and stems it was 20 times. In the males of this strain the figures were eight, nine, two, and three and a half times, respectively. In another Lebanese strain, the female had a nearly 1:1 ratio of CBD to THC in all parts, while the male had one and one tenth times more CBD in the flowers and six, four and 15 times more THC in the top and bottom leaves and stems.

A recent study of marijuana grown in the Netherlands showed that the ratio of CBD to THC was almost constant at 1.3 for all leaves on the plant and for each part of each leaf, except that there was slightly more CBD in the leaf tips of large leaves (mean ratio 1.7). The wide variation discussed above may be partly due to sampling errors, but undoubtedly, as with virtually every other aspect of this extraordinary plant, there is great variation from one strain to another. A study of Turkish plants showed CBD content of 1.7% in the lower parts of single

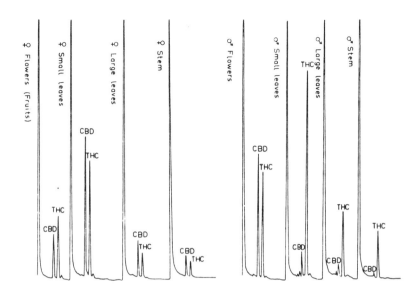

Fig. 14. Gas chromatograms showing cannabinoid content of various parts of male and female Lebanese marijuana. In this example the small (upper) leaves of the male have the highest THC content and most parts of the female have more CBD than THC—a common finding for Lebanese plants. For a more detailed explanation of chromatography see the testing section of this book. (Reprinted from A. Ohlsson et al., *Bulletin on Narcotics,* Vol. 23, 1971.)

small bracts, but only 0.5% in the upper parts of the same bracts. The higher concentration in the lower parts is probably due to the fact that they are older and have had more time to synthesize. Remember that Turkish plants are generally of the high CBD, low THC variety.

One practical consequence of these data is that particular care must be paid to the precise part of the plant being used. In sampling a kilo, for example, you may get a very incorrect impression if you happen to taste some bottom leaves or, conversely, some flowering tips. Another consequence is that the more potent the plant, the more striking the difference between the flowering tops and the leaves.

## TABLE 7
### Cannabinoid Content of Various Plant Parts
*See table 2 for details*

$V_1$ = Vegetative plant of strain 1

3 $M_1$ = Male of strain 1 at 3 months     4 $F_1$ = Female of strain 1 at 4 months, etc.

*(Subscripts designate different plants)*

M,F = Mature plants

| Seed Origin | Grown In | Sex | Compound | Bractlets | Bracts | Pollen | Flowers | LEAVES Top | Mid. | Bot. | Stems |
|---|---|---|---|---|---|---|---|---|---|---|---|
| Japan | Japan | F | THC | | 4.8 | | | 1.9 | | | |
| | | M | THC | | 2.6 | | | 0.6 | | | |
| Turkey | USA (Miss.) | F | THC | | 0.4 | | | 0.3 | | | T |
| | | F | CBD | | 5.5 | | | 1.5 | | | 0.2 |
| Japan | Japan | 4 $F_1$ | THC | 2.2 | 1.9 | | | 3.7* | | 1.3 | |
| | | 4 $F_1$ | CBD | 0.1 | 0.2 | | | 0.1* | | 0.2 | |
| | | 3 $F_1$ | THC | 3.7 | 1.6 | | | 4.0* | | 1.0 | |
| | | 3 $F_1$ | CBD | 0.2 | 0.1 | | | 0.3* | | 0.1 | |
| | | 4 $F_2$ | THC | 2.2 | 1.3 | | | 1.0* | | 0.9 | |
| | | 4 $F_2$ | CBD | 0.7 | 0.3 | | | 0.6* | | T | |
| | | 3 $F_2$ | THC | 1.7 | 0.6 | | | 1.8* | | 0.1 | |
| | | $3_t F_2$ | CBD | 0.2 | 0.1 | | | 0.3* | | T | |

| Seed Origin | Grown In | Sex | Compound | Bractlets | Bracts | Pollen | Flowers | LEAVES | | | Stems |
|---|---|---|---|---|---|---|---|---|---|---|---|
| | | | | | | | | Top | Mid. | Bot. | |
| | | ♂ $M_1$ | THC | | 1.1 | 0.3 | | 1.4* | | 1.0 | 0.1 |
| | | ♂ $M_1$ | CBD | | 0.1 | T | | 0.4* | | 0.1 | T |
| | | ♂ $M_2$ | THC | | 0.6 | 0.1 | | 1.2* | | 0.8 | T |
| | | ♂ $M_2$ | CBD | | 0.2 | — | | 0.3* | | 0.2 | 0.1 |
| Lebanon | Lebanon | F | CBD | | | | 2.4 | 1.1 | 0.3 | | |
| | | M | CBD | | | | 1.3 | 0.6 | 0.4 | | T |
| USSR | Sweden | F | CBD | | | | 0.5 | 0.5 | 0.1 | | |
| | | M | CBD | | | | 0.6 | 0.3 | 0.4 | | T |
| Turkey | Sweden | F | CBD | | | | 0.8 | 0.5 | 0.7 | | |
| | | M | CBD | | | | 0.7 | 0.7 | 0.5 | | T |
| Czech. | Sweden | F | CBD | | | | 0.7 | 0.5 | 0.4 | | |
| | | M | CBD | | | | 0.7 | 0.2 | 0.2 | | T |
| So. Africa | England | F | THC | | | | 1.8-7.1 | 1.3-6.9 | 0.1-4.5 | | |
| | | $F_1$ | THC | | | | | 4.8 | 3.1 | 1.5 | |
| | | $F_2$ | THC | | | | | 6.1 | 3.0 | 0.8 | |
| | | $F_3$ | THC | | | | | 6.9 | 5.5 | 4.0 | |
| | | $F_4$ | THC | | | | 3.7 | 3.0 | | | |
| | | $F_5$ | THC | | | | 3.4 | 1.9 | | | |

| Seed Origin | Grown In | Sex | Compound | Bractlets | Bracts | Pollen | Flowers | LEAVES Top | Mid. | Bot. | Stems |
|---|---|---|---|---|---|---|---|---|---|---|---|
| Thailand | England | F | THC | | | | 2.4 | 0.9 | | | |
| Mexico | USA (Miss.) | F | THC | | 3.7 | | | 1.4 | | | |
| | | M | THC | | | | 1.6 | 1.0 | | | 0.9 |
| Nepal | England | F$_1$ | THC | 5.8 | 1.4 | | | | | | |
| | | | CBD | 3.5 | 0.6 | | | | | | |
| | | F$_2$ | THC | 3.4 | 1.6 | | | | | | |
| | | | CBD | 2.1 | 0.8 | | | | | | |
| Japan | Japan | F | THC | 10.9 | | | | | | | |

*Values are a mixture of flowers and top leaves.

SOURCE: K.H. Davis et al., "The Preparation and Analysis of Enriched and Pure Cannabinoids from Marihuana and Hashish," *Lloydia* 33 (1970): 453; F. Merkus, "Cannabivarin and Tetrahydrocannabivarin, Two Constituents of Hashish," *Nature* 232 (1971): 579; P.S. Fetterman et al., "Mississippi Grown *Cannabis sativa* L.," *Journal of Pharmaceutical Science* 60 (1971): 1246; P. Chambon et al., "Problemes Poses Par la Culture Locale du Chanvre et Dosage des Chanvre," *Bulletin des Traveaux de la Societe de Pharmacie de Lyon* 16 (1972): 46.

# Propyl Cannabinoids

Before 1969 it was thought that all naturally occurring cannabinoids had the pentyl or five carbon side chain in the right
hand (benzenoid) ring. Then some samples were discovered
which contained small amounts of cannabinoids with a propyl
or three carbon side chain instead of the pentyl. The three analogs of CBD, THC and CBN with the propyl side chain are
termed cannabidivarol (CBDV), tetrahydrocannabivarol (THCV)
and cannabivarol (CBV). Samples having significant amounts of
these compounds generally come from India and adjacent areas
(Nepal, Afghanistan, Pakistan), South Africa and Indonesia.
However, it is assumed that further testing will reveal their presence in marijuana from other areas. Small quantities have been
detected in marijuana from 29 countries; only seeds from Morocco, Poland and Turkey yielded plants without at least traces. As
the table below shows, some samples may contain up to 50% of
their cannabinoids as THCV or CBDV. Some South African
plants have as high as 80% of the total cannabinoids present as
THCV. It is presently unknown whether the quantity of these
compounds is affected by age, sex or plant part in any way significantly different from that of the pentyl cannabinoids. The
only relevant data, from South African plants grown indoors,
are presented below. It is apparent that higher temperatures
favor the production of propyl compounds relative to pentyl
and of cannabinoids in the males relative to the females.

|        |      | MALE | FEMALE |
|--------|------|------|--------|
| 32° C  | THC  | 0.19 | 0.16   |
|        | THCV | 0.14 | 0.08   |
| 22° C  | THC  | 0.07 | 0.14   |
|        | THCV | 0.02 | 0.06   |

(Plants grown from South African seeds indoors at
32° C or 22° C for 16-hour light period, then 12° C
for eight-hour dark period.)

It is especially interesting that the duration of action of the
propyl cannabinoids is significantly shorter than that of the
pentyl compounds. Smoking marijuana with large amounts of
THCV should produce a shorter high than usual, but human ex-

## TABLE 8

## Cannabinoids and Propyl Cannabinoids of High Potency Strains

*All values are % of total cannabinoids rounded off to nearest %*

THCV = Tetrahydrocannabivarin   CBDV = Cannabidivarin   T = <1%

### Marijuana

| SEED ORIGIN | GROWN IN | CONDITION | THC | THCV | CBD | CBDV |
|---|---|---|---|---|---|---|
| Afghanistan | USA (Mississippi) | Vegetative | – | 48 | – | T |
| | | Flowering | 67 | 4 | 4 | 10 |
| South Africa | France | Immature | 70 | 17 | – | – |
| South Africa | Indoors | Immature | 65 | 30 | – | – |
| South Africa | USA (Mississippi) | Flowering | – | 54 | – | T |
| India | USA (Mississippi) | Flowering | – | 11 | – | 2 |
| Nigeria | USA (Mississippi) | Vegetative | – | 9 | – | T |
| Indonesia | Indonesia | Flowering | 81 | – | 3 | T |
| | | Flowering | 3 | – | 12 | 50 |
| | | Flowering | 31 | – | 14 | 20 |
| | | Flowering | 70 | – | 6 | 8 |

| SEED ORIGIN | GROWN IN | CONDITION | THC | THCV | CBD | CBDV |
|---|---|---|---|---|---|---|
| Thailand (1971) | Norway | Immature | 80 | — | 9 | — |
| Thailand (1972) | Norway | Immature | 89 | — | 8 | — |
| Turkey (1971) | Norway | Flowering | 3 | — | 96 | — |
| Turkey (1972) | Norway | Flowering | 13 | — | 85 | — |
| South Africa | Norway | Immature | 84 | — | 4 | — |
| South Africa | South Africa | Flowering | 56-92 | — | 3-12 | — |
| Burma | Burma | Flowering | 9-22 | — | 11-25 | — |
| Nigeria | Nigeria | Flowering | 26-78 | — | 4-13 | — |
| Jamaica | Jamaica | Flowering | 55-98 | — | 2-17 | — |
| Morocco | Morocco | Flowering | 45-66 | — | 30-40 | — |

Hashish

| SEED ORIGIN | GROWN IN | CONDITION | THC | THCV | CBD | CBDV |
|---|---|---|---|---|---|---|
| Nepal | Nepal | Flowering | 3-12 | 2-6 | 36-41 | 9-12 |
| Pakistan | Pakistan | Flowering | 15-53 | — | 39-57 | — |
| Lebanon | Lebanon | Flowering | 25-36 | — | 59-66 | — |
| Afghanistan | Afghanistan | Flowering | 42-61 | — | 35-45 | — |

SOURCE: R.W. Jenkins and D.A. Patterson, "The Relationship Between Chemical Composition and Geographical Origin of *Cannabis*," *Forensic Science* 2 (1973): 59; C.E. Turner et al., "Constituents of *Cannabis sativa* L. VI," *Journal of Pharmaceutical Science* 62 (1973): 1739; Mobarak et al., "Studies on Non-Cannabinoids of Hashish. II," *Chemosphere* 3 (1974): 265; C.E. Turner and K.W. Hadley, "Chemical Analysis of *Cannabis sativa* of Distinct Origin," *Archivos Investigacion Medica* 5, supplement (1974): 144; M. Paris et al., "Importance des Composes Propyliques dans le *Cannabis* Originaire d'Afrique du Sud," *Plantes Medicinales Phytotherapie* 9 (1975): 136; K.H. Davis et al., "The Preparation and Analysis of Enriched and Pure Cannabinoids from Marihuana and Hashish," *Lloydia* 33 (1970): 453; F. Merkus, "Cannabivarin and Tetrahydrocannabivarin, Two Constituents of Hashish," *Nature* 232 (1972): 579; P.S. Fetterman et al., "Mississippi Grown *Cannabis sativa* L.," *Journal of Pharmaceutical Science* 60 (1971): 1246; P. Chambon et al., "Problemes Poses Par la Culture Locale du Chanvre et Dosage des Chanvre," *Bulletin des Traveaux de la Societe de Pharmacie de Lyon* 16 (1972): 46.

periments have not yet been reported. For further discussion of chain length and chemical syntheses, see the chemistry section of this book.

## Cannabinoid Content of Female Flowering Tops

It is well known that marijuana from various areas of the world varies considerably in potency, but only very recently has any quantitative data become available. Table 8 gives figures in percent of dry weight for the CBD and THC contents of female flowering tops. The high THC strains are generally found south of latitude 30° North, although there are many exceptions to this. For example, one of the wild Illinois strains contained 2.3% THC. Most wild American hemp has derived from plants that were grown for fiber, and often originated from seeds imported from China in the nineteenth century. Though most Chinese strains are probably of the high THC type, natural selection eventually changed these into the high CBD, low THC type. It should be kept in mind that the figures presented are by no means exhaustive of the range of variation existing in each country, and that in many cases much higher contents would be found if more extensive studies on completely mature plants were done. Also, the recent development of an extensive underground traffic in marijuana has led to seeds of diverse origins being deliberately cultivated or scattered about in nearly every country, so we never know for certain (especially for wild stands) whether the particular plants studies derive from numerous inbred generations or if they are the result of a recent cross with seeds from the other side of the world. Nevertheless, Mississippi researchers found a five-fold variation in THC content of plants derived from seeds from a single plant and, undoubtedly, such variation is neither uncommon nor the maximum. It is likewise reasonable to expect more variation in the offspring if the parents are of different strains.

In spite of these difficulties, the data are probably quite typical for plants from the areas indicated. It should be useful to refer to the section on cannabinoid phenotypes before studying table 8.

One point of immediate interest is the extreme variation in potency of samples from one country. The study on Argentinian plants showed a range of 0.5 to 8.3% THC; that is, from very weak to a quality comparable to the best Colombian or Thai marijuana. Mexican marijuana seized at the border was tested and found to be quite weak. Of 40 batches seized, only ten of them had greater than 1% THC, and the range was 0.7 to 2.87%. Evidently there are still hundreds of tons of Mexican weed being imported which are quite incapable of getting anyone stoned. Presumably they are being bought by teenagers who can't tell the difference between grass and oregano. Even the best of the Mexican marijuana tested was still only half as potent as good Colombian, Jamaican or Thai and, furthermore, had the additional disadvantage of higher CBD content than the latter types. A series of samples analyzed in Jamaica averaged 2.96% THC with a range of 0.7 to 10.3%, the latter figure being the equal of the most potent marijuana grown anywhere. Ten Costa Rican samples varied from 1.0 to 3.7%. Similar variation is observed in the plants of the high CBD type, as in wild Illinois marijuana where the CBD ranges from traces to more than 7%.

There is much speculation as to the maximum potency obtainable from marijuana. THC contents over 8% are seldom found, except for a few unpublished studies which claim ranges up to 15%. Values over 10% must be regarded with suspicion, since there is the possibility that hash oil may have been added. This is especially true of hashish. Sampling error is another serious problem. If a small amount chosen for analysis contains mostly flowers or bractlets, very high values might be obtained, but these would not be truly representative of the whole flowering top. Likewise, samples may be biased toward lower values. To avoid this problem, a thoroughly mixed sample of some two to four grams of material should be extracted and analyzed. It is possible that breeding programs may be able to increase potency beyond that which occurs in nature.

# Thai and Other Southeast Asian Delicacies

It is interesting to note that Thai seeds grown in both England
and Mississippi produced marijuana of good but not remarkable
potency (2.4 and 3.2% THC). Thai grass has sometimes sold for
more than $2000 a pound and up to $30 per stick (enough for
about four joints), but, as with all marijuana, the quality varies
greatly and there is also much bogus Thai around. I have
smoked various batches of homegrown Thai from California and
found it to be of only moderate quality. While it is true that
these different environments and times of harvest have probably
not allowed these seeds to express their full potential for THC
production, it is relevant that some of the South African seeds
grown in the same experiments in England and Mississippi produced plants with over 6% THC. Three samples grown in Thailand had 4.8, 1.3 and 2.1% THC. The most potent Thai tops,
which must have 8 to 10% THC in some cases, have not yet
found their way into official analyses. It is also interesting that
some Thai plants seem to be of the high CBD or at least of the
intermediate type. In the Mississippi study, one plant had 2.4%
CBD and 1.4% THC, but it is possible that if such plants matured fully, the CBD would mostly be converted into THC.

Comparing other Asian strains, two young, nonflowering
Vietnamese plants grown in the same study contained 4.0 and
1.0% THC and only traces of CBD, while a Vietnamese male had
3.2% THC and 0.5% CBD. Four Korean stocks contained only
traces of CBD (except one with 0.4%) and up to 3.8% THC in
the only plants which matured (males). In one Chinese plant, the
female had 2.0% THC and 1.9% CBD. Finally, Japanese plants
are typically of the high THC type with up to 4%, and with a
CBD content ranging from a quarter to nearly equal that of the
THC. Summarizing, we can say that Southeast Asian marijuana
is typically of the high THC type, but that it often contains
sizeable quantities of CBD.

It is also to be kept in mind that Southeast Asian marijuana,
at least when grown there, tends to convert much of the THC
into CBN (this has been termed overripe marijuana). Although
this is generally true of high THC plants even when grown in
cool climates (South African plants grown in Norway had up to

0.8% CBN and 2% THC), the tendency seems to reach its extreme in Southeast Asia. Burmese samples sometimes have more than 60% of their total cannabinoids present as CBN. While these amounts of CBN will probably not be of much significance so far as modifying THC effects is concerned, it does represent a substantial loss of THC. Consequently, in hot, humid areas it is important not to let plants overripen and not to store marijuana for long periods. Finally, we may note that since the conversion of THC to CBN is nonenzymatic, it should depend mostly on the environment, not on the strain of marijuana.

## TABLE 9

**Cannabinoid Content of Female Flowering Tops**
*See table 2 for details*
*Immature plants are young females or, in a few cases,
presumed females. Multiple values for a country represent
different seed stocks*

### High THC Strains (Female ⩾ 0.5%)

| SEED ORIGIN | GROWN IN | CONDITION | THC | CBD |
|---|---|---|---|---|
| Afghanistan | Indoors | Immature | 0.8 | 0.2 |
| Afghanistan | Mississippi | Immature | 2.1 | 0.2 |
| Argentina | Argentina | Flowering | 0.5 | 0.7 |
|  |  | Flowering | 0.9 | T |
|  |  | Flowering | 3.3 | T |
|  |  | Flowering | 8.3 | 0.2 |
| Chile | Canada | Immature | 0.8 | 0.1 |
| China | Mississippi | Immature | 2.0 | 1.9 |
| Colombia | Colombia | Flowering | 5.5 | – |
| Costa Rica | Costa Rica | Flowering | 1.0 | T |
| Czechoslovakia | Czechoslovakia | Flowering | 0.5 | 1.3 |
| Costa Rica | Costa Rica | Flowering | 3.2 | T |
| France | Mississippi | Flowering | 3.2 | 0.1 |
| Gambia | Canada | Immature | 1.0 | 0.1 |

# THC AND CBD CONTENT

| SEED ORIGIN | GROWN IN | CONDITION | THC | CBD |
|---|---|---|---|---|
| Ghana | Mississippi | Immature | 2.6 | T |
| Hawaii | Hawaii | Flowering | 6.9 | – |
| India | India | Flowering | 5.6 | 2.2 |
| | | Flowering | 7.4 | 1.9 |
| India | Mississippi | Flowering | 1.3 | 0.9 |
| Italy | Denmark | Immature | 0.6 | 0.3 |
| Jamaica | Indoors | Immature | 1.3 | 0.1 |
| Japan | Canada | Immature | 1.4 | 0.3 |
| | | Immature | 0.6 | 0.3 |
| Japan | Japan | Flowering | 1.2 | 0.2 |
| | | Flowering | 0.9 | T |
| | | Flowering | 2.1 | – |
| Korea | Mississippi | Flowering | 1.0 | 0.1 |
| Lebanon | Mississippi | Flowering | 1.0 | 2.0 |
| Mexico | Mississippi | Flowering | 3.7 | 0.4 |
| | | Flowering | 1.4 | 0.1 |
| | | Flowering | 1.8 | T |
| | | Flowering | 4.0 | 0.4 |
| Mexico | Acapulco | Flowering | 4.2 | – |
| Nepal | England | Flowering | 2.7 | – |
| | | Flowering | 4.4 | – |
| Nepal | Indoors | Immature | 1.3 | 0.1 |
| | | Flowering | 2.4 | – |
| Netherlands | Canada | Flowering | 1.4 | 0.2 |
| Panama | Panama | Flowering | 3.2 | 0.3 |
| Panama | New Hampshire | Flowering | 4.0 | 0.4 |
| Panama | Panama | Flowering | 5.7 | – |
| Panama | Indoors | Immature | 0.6 | 0.1 |
| Peru | Mississippi | Immature | 2.1 | T |
| Poland | Canada | Flowering | 1.1 | 0.7 |
| Rumania | Canada | Flowering | 0.6 | 1.3 |

| SEED ORIGIN | GROWN IN | CONDITION | THC | CBD |
|---|---|---|---|---|
| Senegal | Mississippi | Immature | 3.6 | 0.1 |
| Sierra Leone | Mississippi | Immature | 1.2 | T |
| South Africa | England | Flowering | 7.1 | – |
|  |  | Flowering | 2.1 | – |
| South Africa | Mississippi | Immature | 6.1 | T |
| South Africa | Denmark | Immature | 1.7 | T |
| South Africa | Norway | Immature | 2.0 | 0.1 |
| South Africa | Czechoslovakia | Immature | 1.3 | – |
| Sweden | Canada | Flowering | 0.9 | 0.6 |
| Thailand | England | Flowering | 2.4 | – |
| Thailand | Thailand | Flowering | 1.3 | 0.1 |
|  |  | Flowering | 4.8 | 0.1 |
| Thailand | Mississippi | Flowering | 3.2 | 0.4 |
|  |  | Flowering | 1.4 | 2.4 |
| Thailand | Czechoslovakia | Immature | 0.6 | 0.1 |
| Turkey | Mississippi | Flowering | 2.8 | 1.9 |
|  | Czechoslovakia | Flowering | 0.1 | 1.1 |
| USA (Iowa) | Mississippi | Flowering | 0.7 | 2.7 |
| USA (Illinois) | Illinois | Flowering | 2.3 | – |
| USA (New Jersey) | New Jersey | Flowering | 0.7 | 0.4 |
| USA (Iowa) | Iowa | Flowering | 0.5 | 0.4 |
| Vietnam | Mississippi | Immature | 4.0 | T |

## Intermediate Strains (Female ⩾ 0.6% THC; Female ⩾ 0.8% CBD)

| SEED ORIGIN | GROWN IN | CONDITION | THC | CBD |
|---|---|---|---|---|
| Czechoslovakia | Canada | Flowering | 0.7 | 0.8 |
| England | Canada | Flowering | 0.6 | 1.5 |
| Germany | Canada | Flowering | 0.6 | 1.4 |
| Greece | Greece | Flowering | 0.7 | 2.8 |
| Hungary | Canada | Flowering | 0.6 | 1.5 |
| India | Canada | Flowering | 0.6 | 0.7 |

| SEED ORIGIN | GROWN IN | CONDITION | THC | CBD |
|---|---|---|---|---|
| Lebanon • | Norway | Immature | 0.8 | 1.0 |
| Lebanon | Mississippi | Flowering | 1.0 | 2.0 |
| Poland | Canada | Flowering | 1.1 | 0.7 |
|  |  | Flowering | 1.3 | 1.2 |
| Rumania | Canada | Flowering | 0.6 | 1.3 |
| Sudan | Mississippi | Flowering | 2.1 | T |
| Sweden | Mississippi | Flowering | 0.9 | 0.6 |
| Thailand | Mississippi | Flowering | 1.4 | 2.4 |
| Turkey | Canada | Flowering | 1.3 | 1.3 |
| USA (Iowa) | Mississippi | Flowering | 0.7 | 2.7 |
| USSR | Canada | Flowering | 0.7 | 1.3 |
| Yugoslavia | Canada | Flowering | 0.6 | 1.0 |

## High CBD Low THC Strains
### (Female ≤ 0.5% THC; Female ≥ 0.6% CBD)

| SEED ORIGIN | GROWN IN | CONDITION | THC | CBD |
|---|---|---|---|---|
| Argentina | Argentina | Flowering | 0.5 | 0.7 |
| Brazil | Brazil | Flowering | 0.1 | 0.6 |
| Canada | Canada | Flowering | T | 2.0 |
|  |  | Flowering | T | 1.0 |
| Cyprus | Canada | Flowering | 0.1 | 0.6 |
| Czechoslovakia | Canada | Flowering | 0.1 | 1.4 |
|  |  | Flowering | 0.1 | 0.8 |
|  |  | Flowering | T | 1.7 |
| England | Canada | Flowering | 0.1 | 2.0 |
|  |  | Flowering | 0.2 | 1.1 |
| France | Canada | Flowering | 0.1 | 2.8 |
|  |  | Flowering | T | 1.9 |
| France | France | Flowering | T | 0.6 |
| Germany | Canada | Flowering | 0.5 | 1.3 |
|  |  | Flowering | 0.1 | 2.7 |

| SEED ORIGIN | GROWN IN | CONDITION | THC | CBD |
|---|---|---|---|---|
| Greece | Greece | Flowering | 0.7 | 2.8 |
| Hungary | Canada | Flowering | 0.5 | 1.5 |
|  |  | Flowering | T | 1.6 |
|  |  | Flowering | 0.1 | 2.5 |
| India | Canada | Flowering | 0.3 | 1.2 |
| Ireland | Canada | Flowering | 0.1 | 0.8 |
| Israel | Canada | Flowering | 0.2 | 1.0 |
|  |  | Flowering | 0.5 | 0.7 |
| Italy | Canada | Flowering | 0.1 | 1.9 |
|  |  | Flowering | T | 2.8 |
|  |  | Flowering | 0.5 | 0.6 |
|  |  | Flowering | 0.3 | 1.2 |
| Lebanon | Mississippi | Flowering | 1.0 | 2.0 |
| Lebanon | Lebanon | Flowering | T | 2.8 |
|  |  | Flowering | 0.5 | 2.4 |
| Mexico | Canada | Flowering | 0.4 | 0.7 |
| Netherlands | Canada | Flowering | 0.1 | 1.3 |
|  |  | Flowering | 0.4 | 2.1 |
| Poland | Canada | Flowering | 0.4 | 0.7 |
|  |  | Flowering | 0.2 | 1.7 |
|  |  | Flowering | T | 1.5 |
| Portugal | Canada | Flowering | 0.2 | 1.3 |
| Rumania | Canada | Flowering | 0.1 | 1.9 |
|  |  | Flowering | T | 1.1 |
| Spain | Canada | Flowering | 0.4 | 2.7 |
| Sweden | Canada | Flowering | 0.3 | 1.4 |
|  |  | Flowering | 0.4 | 2.2 |
| Switzerland | Switzerland | Flowering | 0.1 | 1.6 |
| Syria | Canada | Flowering | 0.1 | 0.8 |
| Turkey | Canada | Flowering | 0.1 | 0.8 |
|  |  | Flowering | 0.1 | 1.2 |

| SEED ORIGIN | GROWN IN | CONDITION | THC | CBD |
|---|---|---|---|---|
| Turkey | Mississippi | Flowering | 0.2 | 1.7 |
| | | Flowering | 0.1 | 1.0 |
| Turkey | Sweden | Flowering | T | 0.8 |
| USA (Kansas) | Kansas | Flowering | T | 0.9 |
| USA (Iowa) | Canada | Flowering | 0.1 | 1.0 |
| USA (Minnesota) | Canada | Flowering | 0.1 | 1.6 |
| USA (Iowa) | Iowa | Flowering | T | 0.9 |
| USA (Illinois) | Illinois | Flowering | – | 7.1 |
| USA (Iowa) | Mississippi | Flowering | 0.1 | 1.2 |
| USA (Minnesota) | Mississippi | Flowering | 0.1 | 1.2 |
| USA (New Jersey) | New Jersey | Flowering | 0.3 | 1.0 |
| USA (Minnesota) | Minnesota | Flowering | 0.4 | 2.7 |
| | | Flowering | 0.2 | 0.8 |
| USA (Massachusetts) | Massachusetts | Flowering | 0.3 | 1.1 |
| USSR | Canada | Flowering | T | 0.6 |
| | | Flowering | 0.1 | 3.4 |
| | | Flowering | 0.4 | 1.6 |
| Yugoslavia | Canada | Flowering | 0.4 | 1.4 |

SOURCE: R.W. Jenkins and D.A. Patterson, "The Relationship Between Chemical Composition and Geographical Origin of *Cannabis*," *Forensic Science* 2 (1973): 59; C.E. Turner et al., "Constituents of *Cannabis sativa* L. VI," *Journal of Pharmaceutical Science* 62 (1973): 1739; Mobarak et al., "Studies on Non-Cannabinoids of Hashish. II," *Chemosphere* 3 (1974): 265; C.E. Turner and K.W. Hadley, "Chemical Analysis of *Cannabis sativa* of Distinct Origin," *Archivos Investigacion Medica* 5, supplement (1974): 144; M. Paris et al., "Importance des Composes Propyliques dans le *Cannabis* Originaire d'Afrique du Sud," *Plantes Medicinales Phytotherapie* 9 (1975): 136; K.H. Davis et al., "The Preparation and Analysis of Enriched and Pure Cannabinoids from Marihuana and Hashish," *Lloydia* 33 (1970): 453; F. Merkus, "Cannabivarin and Tetrahydrocannabivarin, Two Constituents of Hashish," *Nature* 232 (1972): 579; P.S. Fetterman et al., "Mississippi Grown *Cannabis sativa* L.," *Journal of Pharmaceutical Science* 60 (1971): 1246; P. Chambon et al., "Problemes Poses Par la Culture Locale du Chanvre et Dosage des Chanvre," *Bulletin des Traveaux de la Societe de Pharmacie de Lyon* 16 (1972): 46.

# Wild Weed in the USA

As mentioned elsewhere here, wild marijuana in the USA has generally escaped from fiber cultivation and is of the high CBD type. However, there is considerable variation with many intermediate and some high THC stands occurring (see tables). In the U.S., as elsewhere, insufficient study has been done to determine the frequency distribution of the various types within a given country, locality or even a single stand. Most studies have been, incomplete in their sampling and have presented the data in a careless and inadequate fashion. Three detailed reports on wild American hemp have been published. The Illinois study already mentioned found that 101 naturalized stands in that state ranged from 0.15 to 7.1% CBD and from 0.04 to 2.27% THC. Assuming a normal curve, 68% of the stands had between 0.25 1.79% CBD and between 0.03 and 0.65% THC. A Kansas study of ten locations found CBD ranging from 0.12% to 1.7% and THC from 0.01% to 0.49%. There was one and a half to 25 times more CBD than THC in the samples. The CBD content was highest in mid-June and the THC content in early July. The male flowers tended to have a slightly higher cannabinoid content than the female flowers. The plants were about seven feet tall before flowering and about eight and a half feet tall at maturity. The third study, conducted on three different stands in Indiana, found that the CBD content varied over the season from traces to 6.8% and THC content varied from traces to 1.5%.[3]

# Recent Observations
# On Environmental Effects

Although there is a vast older literature on the effects of various environmental manipulations on marijuana, it is of no use for present purposes since the observations usually didn't pertain to cannabinoid content. Even when they did, there were no good tests for quantitative measurement of the active compounds.

The studies on wild hemp in Illinois and Indiana attempted to correlate many factors of soil content with cannabinoid production, but nothing conclusive emerged. Both studies agreed that environmental variables which stressed the plants resulted in increased cannabinoid content. By far the most carefully controlled study was done in 1975 on Afghani plants grown in a greenhouse. All the variables were kept constant except the soil: 11 distinct types native to Maryland were used. At six weeks, before the plants flowered, they were harvested and their cannabinoids measured. THC exceeded CBD for all soils except one which was somewhat higher than average in potassium and lower in calcium. Since this one exception had a low total cannabinoid content, the conclusion was that deficient soil retarded development and conversion of CBD to THC. In the study, the CBD content did not vary significantly but THC varied by a factor of seven, exceeding CBD from slightly more than one to about six times. The two soils which produced plants with twice as much THC content as the other nine soils, had low magnesium, low iron and a lightly acid pH, and these plants tended to be short, have a low dry weight, a low number of nodes, a small number of leaflets per leaf at the top node, and a fairly high CBD content. Although the plants were immature and quite small when harvested, the data obtained are quite consistent with those of other experiments and there seems no reason to doubt them.

This study provides an excellent illustration of a fundamental point which has escaped its authors as well as everyone else in the field. If we calculate the *total* THC content per plant we find that the two soil conditions which yielded plants with two to three times more total THC than any of the other were actually not those giving the most potent plants. In fact, the plants with the greatest total yield had less than half the THC concentration of the most potent plants. This difference might have been even more striking if the plants had been allowed to mature. Though the *total* THC yield varied by a factor of nine, it might have varied more if mature flowering tops had been obtained. The soil conditions and plant characteristics for maximum *total* yield were strikingly different from those for greatest potency. The two soils had a slightly acid pH, and high phosphate, potassium and calcium, and the plants were the tallest, with the highest number of leaflets per leaf at the top node, the greatest number of nodes, the greatest dry weights and low to moderate CBD levels. The explanation for this may be that stress (in this case soil deficiencies) inhibits the synthesis of proteins, carbohy-

drates, etc. to a greater degree than it inhibits cannabinoid production and thus will give smaller, but more potent plants. If
other kinds of stress, absent from this study but present in nature, were applied, the variation would doubtless be even more
extreme. These would include drought, low light, competition
from other plants, and damage by the elements, insects and
fungi. Even so, the minimal soil stresses in this study led to the
most potent plants being less than half as tall as the plants with
greatest total yield.

The consequences of these observations for the marijuana
farmer are clear. You have two basic choices: high potency and
low yield or lower potency and higher yield. These choices exist
whether you are growing in a closet or in a field. If you have
seeds of consistent quality, a few years' experience should
enable you to manipulate the potency and yield of your product. You might, for example, try to grow 4 kg of 1% THC
weed rather than 1 kg of 2% THC weed, since you could extract
the THC in the former and produce 1 kg of 4% weed. Finally,
don't think that there is a single set of conditions which will
give the greatest total yield or the highest potency, since there
are doubtless many variations in light, soil, water and temperature which will affect the results. Furthermore, these conditions
will vary considerably with the type of seed. These considera-
tions also apply to high CBD type plants, in case you are con-
templating isomerization of CBD to THC (see chapter on isomerization).

A dramatic demonstration of the difference between potency and yield was made in a study done in England. Plants were
grown for about ten weeks and divided into two groups. One
group continued to receive normal lighting, while the other was
placed in the dark for the next three weeks. At the end of this
period, both groups contained approximately the same percentage of cannabinoids, but the plants in the light had doubled in
weight and in total content of cannabinoids. This study also
demonstrated that supplementing the normal greenhouse daylight with either normal or ultraviolet light failed to increase
THC content. The control plants grown outside had the most
THC of all–50% more THC than the plants grown indoors.
Nevertheless, it should be remembered that increasing the light
probably increased total yield.

Several studies which used controlled growth chambers, where conditions can be regulated very precisely, have given interesting results. In one of these, South African seeds yielded more potent plants, particularly in males, when grown at 32° C than at 22° C; but humidity also varied. Another such study used four different types of seeds—two from temperate climates (Illinois and Nepal), and two from tropical climates (Panama and Jamaica), with the Illinois being of the high CBD type and the others of the high THC type. All four types were essentially identical in their ability to increase photosynthesis as the light increased and none saturated even at 120,000 lux (a measure of light intensity). This probably means that no matter what type of seeds you use, you can give the plants as much light as possible for best growth. Half the plants were grown under warm conditions (32° C day and 23° C night) and half under cool conditions (23° C day and 16° C night). When tested at various temperatures, such as might arise during the growing season, plants grown in warm temperatures had higher photosynthetic rates than plants from the cool temperatures. The Illinois plants had the highest photosynthetic rate, with the Nepal intermediate, and Jamaica and Panama being lowest, approximately constant and nearly equal to each other at each test temperature from 20° to 30° C. The chlorophyll contents of the Nepal and Illinois plants were.between four and seven times higher than those of the two tropical groups—a probable factor in the tendency of marijuana from southern areas to be less green when dried. What this data seems to mean is that marijuana from temperate climates, where light is less intense and fall days and growing season shorter, is genetically adapted to produce more rapid growth than that from tropical areas. A corollary to this is that there is probably no way to significantly speed up growth of seeds from tropical areas, though exposing females to a few short days (e.g. eight hours of light) will induce early flowering.

The cannabinoid concentrations were always greater for all four types under cool conditions of growth, but total yield of cannabinoids was probably greater in the warm conditions. Nepalese and Jamaican plants had three to four times greater THC concentrations in the cool temperatures, while Illinois plants had six times more and Panamanian plants were about equal. The first three populations doubled their CBD in the cool temperatures, but the Panamanian plants were again about equal. Unfortunately, all these plants were immature, and the results may have been considerably different if they had been allowed to flower. In cool temperatures, the vegetative leaves had the following THC contents: Illinois, 0.3%; Nepal, 1.3%; Jamaica, 1.3%; and Panama, 0.6%. Thus, American marijuana growers might get much more potent plants from Jamaican seeds than from Panamanian or Colombian seeds, but again, the total yield from the less potent plants might well be significantly greater. These data show once again that there is no precise correlation between plant size or speed of growth and potency. Conditions which give the best growth and the greatest total yield of plant material, and hence of cannabinoids, will usually be different from those giving the most potent marijuana.

Another growth chamber study of the pollen of South African plants found that THC content was maximal when the temperature was maintained at 24° C all the time. With 16 hours at 22° C and eight hours at 12° C (a common situation in temperate areas), the THC content was one-fifth; at 27° C for 24 hours, the yield was one-tenth; and at 32° C for 16 hours, then 12° C for eight hours (areas where it is very warm during the day but cool at night), the yield was 1/20th of that of the 24° C/ 24-hour regimen. In practical terms, this seems to indicate that the strongest marijuana should result from growing at a constant but moderate temperature, and that indoor cultivation should be done in a thermostated room. This can be achieved by leaving the light on for 24 hours a day, which will also produce the maximum growth rate. Furthermore, since research indicates that low night temperatures tend to produce intersexuality (male flowers on female plants), once flowering has been induced by a few short days (e.g., ten hours of light per day for five days), the plants can be returned to constant, 24-hours-a-day light in order to avoid production of male flowers on female plants with the resulting self-fertilization and ruining of sinsemilla. On the other hand, low night temperatures might be used to produce intersexuality and self-fertilization in those cases where it might be desirable to obtain mostly female seeds. To sum up, constant light can be used to maintain moderate to high temperatures, which may achieve maximum THC content, as well as maximum growth rate and avoidance of intersexuality.

Again, maximum total yield of THC will probably not be obtained under the conditions which give the strongest product.

The studies described here demonstrate that stress of almost any kind will tend to produce smaller but more potent plants. Some preliminary data show that plants grown in sand or in shady areas also have somewhat higher THC contents, so these evidently are stress conditions also. While slight nutrient deficiencies may increase potency, recent data show that plants grown under extreme deficiency of nitrogen, potassium and phosphorus, though dwarfed, were comparable to controls in potency. This indicates that there is a point at which stress inhibits cannabinoid production as much as general plant growth, resulting in both low yield and no potency increase.[4]

## Hybrids

Hemp breeders have long known that *Cannabis* strains can easily be crossed with each other. What they don't know is the relative fertility of the second generations. Researchers recently crossed 38 strains representing each of the five cannabinoid types and found that all of the hybrids had the normal diploid number of chromosomes ($2n = 20$), normal meiosis (division of the chromosomes during sexual reproduction), completely strainable pollen (a criterion for fertility), and no chromosomal aberrations. The hybrids were also exceptionally vigorous (a frequent observation when crossing strains of plants) and so there are apparently no breeding barriers between different populations. However, the definitive test of the fertility of the hybrids will be their ability to produce fertile seeds, and all populations have not been tested for interfertility.

The ratios of THC to CBD in the hybrids of the 38 strains were usually about intermediate between those of the parents, but occasionally one of the parents would dominate, with the domination being sometimes for high and sometimes for low THC levels. Three generations of Mexican marijuana grown in Mississippi remained high in THC and low in CBD, but probably most of the crossing was with other Mexican plants. In contrast, third generation Turkish plants had about four times as much THC and roughly half as much CBD as the first generation, indicating that crossing with high THC strains was occurring. Clandestine growers in the midwestern U.S. have found that crossing the wild, low THC type marijuana native to the area with Mexican strains produces spindly, weak plants that seldom mature properly. However, crossing the native plants with red or gold Colombian produced marijuana with about one half the THC content of the Colombian, which matured and gave fertile seeds. I have not yet heard about the results of backcrosses of these hybrids with Colombian. They will probably give even higher THC content, though they will probably require a long growing season to mature and will have to be grown indoors if seeds are desired.

It is probable that whatever factors selected for high CBD, low THC type plants in northern latitudes will eventually defeat any attempt to breed a high THC type that matures there, and high THC type seeds will have to continually be imported. Likewise, the attempt of certain governments to breed a variety free from cannabinoids is probably futile. Even if a cannabinoid-free variety should be developed, it would probably be at a severe disadvantage relative to the high cannabinoid types and could never replace them in the wild.

In general, the hybrids can be expected to show the phenomenon of hybrid vigor. This is a common occurrence in plants and merely refers to the fact that when two strains of a species are crossed, the offspring often are more vigorous (i.e., they grow faster, are larger and healthier looking) than either parent. The implications of this for cannabinoid yield are presently unclear.[5]

# 4

# Variations in Content of Noncannabinoids

## Essential Oils

Inevitably, all chemical constituents of marijuana will vary with such factors as genetics, age, sex, and growth conditions. But little research has been done on compounds other than the cannabinoids. The relatively volatile, low molecular weight substances which give plants their characteristic odors can be steam distilled to yield a generally fragrant, oily mixture termed an essential (from essence) oil. About 10% of the contents of the glandular hairs which produce most of the cannabinoids is comprised of the terpene hydrocarbons which make up most of the essential oil. The presence of a high concentration of these compounds in the hairs is yet another bit of evidence to support the notion that they are the biogenetic precursors of the cannabinoids. However, they are likely to be found in significant amounts throughout the cells of the leaves. It should be kept in mind that just as only very small amounts of cannabinoids appear in the essential oil, so will the terpenoids vary in their volatility; that is, the percent of a given compound in the essential oil is not necessarily a precise indicator of its percent of the terpenoids in the intact leaf.

The total yield of essential oil varies between 0.05 and 0.11%, with females and mature plants giving higher yields, at least in some strains. As they are the biogenetic precursors of cannabinoids, the terpenoid contents might be expected to parallel that of the cannabinoids. Males and females seem to have all the same terpenoids (a dozen or so can be easily detected), but the percentage of any given one relative to the others seems to vary at random, with males having more of some and females having more of others. Furthermore, the ratios of the different compounds vary in the different plant

parts, with myrcene (for example) being 3.2% of the oil from
female flowers, but only 0.8% of that from female leaves,
whereas the figures were 6.0 and 1.1% for males (in one study).
Corresponding figures for another constituent were 0.6 and
1.6% for females and 1.3 and 0.5% for males. What all this boils
down to is that there seems to be no precise correlation between any given terpenoid in the oil and the cannabinoids, and
there is probably little hope for establishing any solid correla-
tions of terpenoids with sex, age or seed strain. Nevertheless, we
all know that even taking account of variations in curing, the
aroma and taste of marijuana varies greatly. Furthermore, the
very striking minty odor emitted by some varieties while growing has often been noted. The cannabinoids do not produce the
characteristic smell of marijuana when burned, so the essential
oils are probably responsible. Besides the caryophyllenes, beta-
farnesene, alpha-selinene, beta-phellandrene, limonene and piperidine contribute to the smell of fresh marijuana. Finally, we
note once again that there is no evidence that terpenoids have
any role in psychic effects of marijuana.[1]

## Saturated Hydrocarbons

Short chain saturated hydrocarbons such as propane (three carbon atoms) and butane (four carbon atoms) are familiar to
everyone, but every organism contains small amounts of hydrocarbons with longer chains (more carbon atoms). *Cannabis* is
one of many plants with easily detectable amounts of saturated
hydrocarbons which have between 25 and 30 carbon atoms per
chain. Limited study of these compounds indicates that they
show no consistent variation with growth conditions or cannabinoid content. For example, in comparing two high THC types
(Thai and South African) with a high CBD type (Turkish), it
was found that either or both of the high THC types could be
higher, lower, or about equal to the Turkish strain with respect
to any one of ten different hydrocarbons, in an apparently random fashion. Likewise, when Brazilian seeds were grown in both
Germany and Brazil, it was found that some compounds increased and some decreased in Germany. A survey of a wide
variety of samples from around the world showed that some

hydrocarbons varied greatly and others varied little. For example, normal pentacosane (25 carbons) ranged from traces in Brazilian samples to 4.3% of the total hydrocarbons in Greek marijuana, while normal nonacosane (29 carbons) varied by only about 30% between any two samples. Much further research will be required to determine whether there is any special significance to these variations.[2]

# Alkaloids

Most of the plant chemicals found in nature which have any striking physiological effects at low dose levels are alkaloids; that is, they are nitrogen-containing compounds with basic (as opposed to acidic) properties. Consequently, it was surprising to find that the active constituent of marijuana was not an alkaloid. Nevertheless, all organisms contain numerous alkaloids in small quantities and a few of these have been isolated in marijuana. The relatively complex alkaloid, cannabisativine, constitutes about 0.001% of the leaves and 0.0005% of the roots of Thai plants, but seems to be absent or present only in traces in high CBD type plants; while the simple alkaloid, hordenine, seems to have an opposite pattern of distribution. Unlike the other constituents discussed here, the alkaloids seem to be correlated with the cannabinoids, at least in the high THC strains. For a high CBD strain, the conditions giving highest CBD concentrations were different from those giving highest alkaloids, but these data are very preliminary. It is extremely unlikely that alkaloids are of any significance as far as marijuana psychoactivity is concerned.[3]

# Variations in the Opiate Content of Poppies

In order to help place in proper perspective the mass of data on variations in chemical constituents of marijuana, it may be helpful to very briefly consider some data that have been obtained on opium poppies. There are many strains of poppies which vary greatly in their total yield of opium alkaloids, as well as in their content of any particular alkaloid. In one variety studied in the

U.S.S.R., the content of morphine and codeine each varied by a factor of two, and growing conditions which increased morphine decreased codeine. Morphine content decreased as one moved from southern to northern latitudes, while codeine and percentage of total alkaloids increased, but total yield of alkaloids was greatest in the southern latitudes. Evidently, as with cannabinoids, the opium alkaloids increase relatively (i.e., in percent by weight) in response to stress, but total yield is highest when stress is minimal. Likewise, it was discovered that whereas green capsules had the highest morphine concentration five to seven days after flowering, mature, dry capsules collected 33 to 35 days after flowering had the highest total morphine content. A crop yielded 25% more morphine if harvested when mature than at the earlier stage. It was also found that there was 20% greater total yield if the plants were spaced 6 cm apart rather than 12 or 18 cm. Finally, as with *Cannabis,* it has been found that the seeds do not contain the active constituents.[4]

# 5

# Harvesting and Preparing Marijuana and Hashish

## Scientific Foundations

To obtain maximum potency, the timing of the harvest is critical. Sometime after the seed has become fully mature, the plant will begin to senesce and die. THC production begins to decrease and THC begins to degrade into CBN (this happens in the living plant as well as after harvest). Unfortunately, a reliable, scientifically-proven method of determining exactly when to harvest in order to maximize THC and minimize CBD has yet to be developed.

One approach is to harvest the plants continually by pinching off or pruning the flowering tops. Another is to cut them back severely to within a foot or so of the ground, leaving some leafy branches, which are removed several weeks later when the new branches have sprouted. Outdoor growers who have to deal with climatic fluctuations tend to harvest their whole crop as soon as it's mature, but in areas where the climate remains mild, large outdoor crops can also be harvested continually for as long as six months.

Farmers in Asia sometimes bend the stem of the plant near the base or cut it and insert a small stone or a piece of opium a few days before harvest. They believe that this will increase its potency, but there are no reliable data on this point, and there is no apparent mechanism by which potency increase could occur. After harvesting, it is common practice to hang the cut plants upside down for curing. These and other methods may rest on the mistaken belief that cannabinoids are synthesized in the roots and translocated to the top of the plant. This is not true. Actually, the specialized cells which synthesize cannabinoids happen to be more numerous and perhaps more active in the flowering tops than elsewhere.

Most descriptions of the preparation of *Cannabis* products are second-hand repeats of nineteenth century accounts—none too accurate to begin with. The accounts generally derive from India and adjacent areas and use the native terms for the products. Since the procedures they describe are the world's oldest for the preparation of *Cannabis* products, it is appropriate to recount a few of them here. Most are from the *Indian Hemp Drugs Commission Report* (1893-1894).

## Harvesting and Hashmaking in India

The terms *charas, ganja* and *bhang* are roughly equivalent to hashish, flowering tops and leaves, respectively. As will be seen, the preparation methods vary considerably.

> The manufacture of round ganja is not completed till the fourth day after the plants are cut. The plants are gathered somewhat later in the day and laid out under the open sky for the night. The sorting is done the next morning, a great deal more of the woody portion being rejected than in the case of flat ganja. The twigs are laid out in the sun till noon, when the men return to the "chator" and rolling is begun. A horizontal bar is lashed on to uprights about four feet from the ground, and mats are placed on the ground on each side of it. Bundles of twigs, either tied together by the stem ends or not, according to the skill of the treader, are set out on the mats. The men range themselves on each side of the bar, and, holding on to it for support, proceed to roll the bundles with their feet. One foot is used to hold the bundle and the other to roll it, working down from the stems to the flower heads. This process goes on for about ten minutes, and during it the bundles are taken up and shaken from time to time to get rid of leaf. The bundles are then broken up and the twigs exposed to the sun. A second but shorter course of rolling by foot follows, and then the twigs are hand pressed, four

or five together. After this the twigs are opened up
and exposed to the sun again. Towards evening the
twigs are made into bundles of about one hundred,
and placed on mats and covered up for the night.

The next morning the bundles are untied and
the twigs again exposed to the sun. If they are sufficiently dry by midday, they only require a little
handling and rolling to complete the manufacture.
If they are not dry enough, the first course of rolling has to be repeated, after which the useless
leaves fall off with a very little manipulation. The
twigs are next sorted according to length and tied
into bundles of three descriptions—short, medium
and long. In this process all useless twigs and sticks
are eliminated. The bundles are placed in rows under a mat which is kept down by a bamboo, and
left for the night. The manufacture is completed
the next day by exposing the bundles to the sun,
heads upwards till the afternoon, and then searching them with hands and bits of stick for any leaves
that may have remained in them. These are shaken
out, and with them pieces of the compressed flower heads, which have been accidentally broken off,
fall on to the mats.

It has been seen that a great quantity of stick,
leaf and seed, and not a little flower head, have
been separated from the bundles of prepared ganja.
The stick may be used as fuel. The leaf is winnowed
from the seed and thrown away, though it has been
proved by analysis to contain the narcotic principle
in larger quantity than ordinary bhang. The seeds
are kept for the next year's culture, and the super-
fluity may find its way into the market. The seeds
are not narcotic and they are sometimes eaten, besides being used for the expression of oil and other
purposes. The bits of flower head are, in the case
of flat ganja, picked up and pressed into the mass
of the flower heads again or burnt . . . In the case
of round ganja, they form the "chur" or "frag-

ments" on which the excise tariff imposes the highest duty, because in that state the drug is absolutely free of leaf and stick.

Bhang as recognized by the excise department
is the dried leaf of the wild plant. . . The preparation consists simply in drying the leaves. The plants
are cut in April . . . but goes on up to June and
July. They are laid out in the sun and one day may
be sufficient to dry them so as to allow the leaves
to be shaken off or beaten off. . . The early flowering stage would seem to be that in which the plant
yields the best bhang.

The method of preparing Khandwa ganja . . .
The harvest begins in the first or second week of
November. The flower heads, which the cultivators
call *mal,* or produce, are broken off with about
twelve inches of twig, carried in baskets to the
threshing floor, and spread out on it in a layer nine
to twelve inches thick . . . The crop is exposed to
the dew for the night. The next day the twigs are
formed into heaps, and each heap is trodden in
turn and when not being trodden is turned over
and exposed to the sun to dry. This goes on for
four or five days and results in the twigs being
pressed flat and deprived of a great portion of their
leaves and thoroughly dried. The produce is then
removed to the cultivator's house, where it is built
into a stack five or six feet high, and has heavy
weights placed upon it.

In the Javadi hills, the plants are cut and carried bodily to the village threshing floor. There
they are sorted, the flower spikes and upper leaves
being retained and the sticks thrown away. The selected heads are spread out for three to five hours
in the heat of the day to dry and are then loosely
rolled in the hand to work out such seed as may
have been formed and to break up the leaf that remains. This working also causes the spikes to stick

to one another to some extent. The broken leaf is then winnowed out, collected and powdered. The flower heads are then placed in a thin layer in a basket which has been dusted within with leaf powder and are trodden by one or two men according to the size of the basket. After the operator has passed over the layer four or five times, it is dusted with leaf powder, and a fresh layer of spikes is put into the basket on top of the other, and the treading is repeated. This process goes on till the basket is full. The contents are then turned out onto flat hard ground and a stone is placed on the pile with other stones to add to the weight. The material is left thus for the night. Next morning, each layer is taken off separately, broken up and spread in the sun. Each piece is trodden and turned over from time to time. In the evening the pieces are again re-piled and weighted for the night, and the next day the process of exposure is repeated until the material is thoroughly dry. Great importance is attached to the thoroughness of the treading, the sufficiency of the pressing, and the completeness of the drying; the quality of the drug being said to depend on the manner in which those processes are carried out. If the latter are not dried sufficiently, they appear green and are of inferior quality, good ganja being brown.

. . . the dried leaves which have fallen out in the process are used as bhang or patti. After carefully removing the stalks, the dried leaves are boiled in water for some time; and the boiled leaves are carefully squeezed with the hands to purge them of all filth and dirt and then dried in the sun. The dried leaves are next boiled either in milk or cocoanut water. The quantity of milk or cocoanut water must be proportionate to the quantity of leaves boiled, so that the milk or cocoanut water might be entirely absorbed by the leaves. They are again

kept in the hot sun for about three or four days.
After they are well dried, they are preserved in
earthen vessels for use.

Charas—This is locally a by-product which is
not brought into account, but appears to be the
harvester's perquisite, who probably part with it to
friends who smoke, if they don't want it themselves.
It is the resinous substance that sticks to the hands
or collects on the sickle when cutting or plucking
the tops. The hands are now and then rubbed together and the charas is collected in the shape of a
pill, which is naturally half dirt and sweat and half
charas. A piece about the size of a marble may perhaps be the reward of a day's work.

. . . from the Upper Sind Frontier . . . charas is
collected by people walking to and fro through the
bhang plants with greased leather coats on and also
by going clothed only in a loincloth with their
bodies smeared with oil. The latter process is followed . . . in the Native States of India. One of the
witnesses also mentions a process resembling that
noticed in the Punjab, by which the dust made by
beating the plant is collected on cloth. He states
that this process is peculiar to Afghanistan: and the
charas from there is well known for its pale green
colour, and is highly appreciated.

It will be seen from the above detailed description that bhang, whether produced by the cultivated or wild plant, is prepared by simple drying.
The processes by which ganja is prepared consist of
pressing, drying, and removal of the leaf. The manufacture is most perfect in Bengal. In other provinces
it is not characterized by the same degree of care
and one or another of the three essential features
of the manufacture is more or less neglected. Ganja
collected from the wild plant and from the bhang
crops of Sind, and probably also that yielded by
stray cultivation, is simply dried. There are only

two methods of preparing charas which appear to
be used when the drug is produced on any considerable scale, *viz.* that by rubbing the flower heads
with the hands as in Kumaon and Nepal, and that
described as being practiced in Yarkand, which
may be called the *garda* method, and consists of
heating the plant over cloth, and manipulating the
dust that is thus deposited. The collection of the
resin adhering to hands and implements in the
course of harvesting ganja is worth remembering,
for it is proved in Gwalior and Bombay. The practice of the Malwa Bhils is perhaps established. Other
methods are unimportant, and the common report
that charas is collected by men dressed in leather
moving about in the hemp crops has not been definitely located. It is doubtful if this device is employed anywhere in India.

In the "Punjab Products" the manufacture of
this sort of charas called *garda* is described. The
finest quality is when the dust is of a reddish colour.
This is called *surkha*. When it is green it is called
*bhangra*. The most inferior is that which adheres to
the cloth after shaking, and has to be scraped off or
shaken off with more violence. This is called *khaki*.
In each case the dust has to be kneaded with a
small quantity of water into a cake, and then forms
charas. It is stated that this drug is much in use. The
specimens which formed the basis of the article
were none of them from the plain districts of the
Punjab, except possibly one from Dera Ghazi Khan.
They came from Lahoul, Spiti, Bokhara, Yarkand,
Dera Ghazi Khan, and Kashmir.

Samples of Baluchistan charas made in the Sara-
wan division of the Kalat State have been sent to
the Indian museum by Mr. Hughes-Buller. The following is the mode of preparation. The female
"bhang" plants are reaped when they are waist high
and charged with seed. The leaves and seeds are

separated and half dried. They are then spread on a carpet made of goat's hair, another carpet is spread over them and slightly rubbed. The dust containing the narcotic principle falls off, and the leaves, etc. are removed to another carpet and again rubbed. The first dust is the best quality, and is known as *nup;* the dust from the second shaking is called *tahgalim,* and is of inferior quality. A third shaking gives *gania* of still lower quality. Each kind of dust is made into small balls called *gabza* and kept in cloth bags. The first quality is recognized by the ease with which it melts. *Nup* is sometimes spelled *rup* and *gania* often given as *gauja.*

A modern visitor to Kashmir noticed two kinds of hashish currently being made: the relatively weak *gurda* made from flowering tops, and *uter* made from the resin and commonly adulterated with clarified butter *(ghee).* Farmers may allow you to rub resin from their plants for 25 cents an ounce. Some persons believe that the sun brings out the resin, but it is more likely that it merely makes it sticky and easier to collect. Place both hands together flat and rub up the top of the plant gently so as not to kill it, spending a few minutes on each plant. After a while, rubbing the hands together will rub off small pieces of hashish. These will be difficult to smoke at first but will become harder as they dry. Modern *gurda* preparation involves shaking, crushing or beating the dried tops over a fine cloth through which the hairs pass. The collected resin is placed in a corn husk, put in the fire for a few seconds and then twisted into a sticky bar about eight inches long and one inch wide.[1]

Still another description of hashish in India is given by Bouquet. He maintains that *bhang* can be made of any combination of leaves and male and/or female flowers, often ground to a coarse powder, which may keep three to four years if protected from sun and moisture. The mixture is incorporated in many preparations such as *buengh* or *poust* (with water) and *lutki* (with alcohol). *Lutki* with opium or *Datura* added is called *mudra.* Bouquet describes three kinds of ganja preparation.

Flat Ganja—the cut stalks are tied together in
bundles, the large leaves are eliminated, and only
the inflorescences, which are stuck together by
the exuded resin, are kept. The bundles of inflorescences are placed on the ground and tramped underfoot to flatten them. The bundles are then untied,
and the product sorted and packed under the name
of large flat or ewig-flat, according to the length
and breadth of the stems.

Round Ganja—instead of being trampled underfoot,
the tops are rolled in the hands until they have become rounded and tapered in shape. This kind of
ganja is always packed in bundles (generally of
twenty-four pieces).

Chur-ganja or Rora—the tops, detached intention-
ally from the plants, or accidentally from the flat
or round ganja, constitute what is known as rora.
This is generally delivered to the consumer in the
form of a coarse powder.[2]

# Hashmaking in Lebanon

In 1932, Lys described the preparation of hashish in Lebanon,
specifically in the areas of Zahle, Ras-Balbeck and Homs. Sometime between August and November, depending mainly on
when the seeds were originally sown, the females are harvested
and left for a week in the open air. The plants are then placed
in the shade for further drying. When dry, the tops are shaken
and gently beaten over a cloth. The resultant powder is sieved
to eliminate the larger pieces of stem and the seeds. The highest
quality is that obtained from the first shaking (hashish zahra or
*zahret el kolch),* which is brown. The remaining powder is
placed in small cloth bags and steamed. The resin melts partially
and is pressed into the desired shape, usually foot-shaped pieces
called soles or *turbahs.* Second quality *(zahret el assa)* is light
brown, and the more crumbly third and fourth qualities are
greenish yellow or green.[3]

# Hashmaking in China

I.C. Chopra and R.N. Chopra, the Indian marijuana experts, have said that the highest yield and best quality charas (hashish) comes from the western area of Sinkiang province near the town of Yarkand. It may still be produced there, since a recent visitor to China reported legally purchasing hash and hashpipes and seeing old people getting stoned in the parks.

There, the plant grows at altitudes up to 5000 feet and reaches ten feet in height. At maturation (September and October), the female flower tops are collected and dried, then crushed between the hands into a powder which is passed through seives until it has the consistency of fine sawdust. This greenish powder is stored in rawhide bags during the four or five months of the winter. At the onset of hot weather, the powder is exposed to the sun long enough for the resin to melt. The resin is stored for a few days in 10- to 14-pound leather bags and then kneaded with wooden rods until each bag yields one to two pounds of the oil, which appears on the surface of the kneaded resinous mass. The charas is then transferred to hide bags for sale. As in other areas, cloth bags may be substituted for rawhide ones and steam may be used to melt the resin.[4]

# Hashmaking in Greece

A report by Brotteaux in 1934 describes a different process used by the Greeks. According to him the males were weeded out as soon as they were recognizable. When the females were fully mature and the basal leaves began to yellow, they were harvested and dried. The flowering tops were crushed between two pieces of linen which yielded a resinous powder, then placed in white linen bags and squeezed in a press. The press produced flattened cakes with the mark of the fabric on them. The preparation of hashish in Greece was described by Rosenthaler in 1911. At that time plants were grown only in the Tripolis area, since neighboring areas had failed to yield potent material. About three to four million kgs were obtained each year. Rosenthaler says nothing about separating males and that the product, in contrast to that from

India, was full of seeds. Seeds were sown in February and March and harvested at the end of August. The plants were cut, bundled and placed in the open to dry for two to three months. Then the seeds and stems were separated and the stems were burnt and used as fertilizer. In December and January the entire harvest was turned into hashish in factories employing 80 to 100 workers each. They collected the dried bundles and beat them with sticks to yield a powder, then sifted through a series of sieves in a tiresome and expensive process. Only 10% of the original material became hashish. Most of that was exported by devious routes to Egypt.[5]

# Hashmaking in Mexico

Oaxacan *pelo rojo*                    Young plant

Sticks removed by hand

Screening seeds

Cleaned weed

Silk-covered bowl

Silk-screening          The results of silk-screening

The powder is poured into a plastic bag for sun drying.

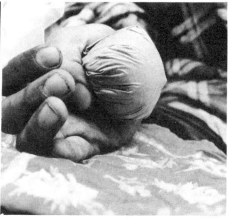

A few grams of the powder are poured into another bag. This is then rolled into a tight ball.

A cloth handkerchief is tightly wrapped around the plastic ball.

The ball is hand twisted and then compressed.

The *mariguano's* hands are moistened with water.

The water is squeezed into the handkerchief-covered ball.

The hash ball is heated over hot coals, slowly.

The final product

# Potent Preparations for
# Smoking, Drinking and Eating

For thousands of years *Cannabis* has been made into a variety of beverages, foodstuffs and, since the sixteenth century, smoking preparations. It has been commonplace, especially in smoking mixtures, to add other potent psychoactive drugs. The possible additive or synergistic (producing a different or greater effect together than alone) effects of these combinations have not been studied. Opium and the leaves of various Solanaceae (tobacco, henbane, Datura), the latter containing scopolamine type compounds (jimsonweed), have been frequent additives. The *anassa* or *nassa* formerly used in Russia was probably of this type. The *hashish kafur* used in the East contained opium and a sweet-smelling substance mixed with powdered hashish and rolled into thin sticks five to ten cm long for smoking.

The drinking preparations are of two main types. For *assis,* one grinds the leaves or tops in a mortar with water and consumes the whole thing. For the *esrar* type, one macerates the leaves with alcohol mixed with syrups or jams diluted with water of roses, jasmine or orange blossom. *Bers* (or *berch*), *chastig* and *chats-raki* (anise scented) are of the *esrar* type. A preparatioɩ of this sort was very popular among underworld people in the Krasnodar area of Russia in the 1930's.

Not surprisingly, most of the eating preparations contained large quantities of honey or sugar. *Manzul* contains about 10% hashish mixed with sesame oil (and often cocoa butter), powdered chocolate, spices and seasonings. A wide variety of crushed or chopped nuts or seeds may be added, and the thick paste is often cut up into flat discs one cm thick and three cm across. Hashish is sometimes added to the *helwa (haloua, heloua)* type of confection so popular in the Middle East. These sweets are characterized as aphrodisiacs in Arab medicine—with opium, cantharides (Spanish fly) and seeds of *Strychnos nux-vomica* containing strychnine frequently added. *Maʾagun* is very similar except that honey and then gum arabic powder are added to form a paste which is made into pellets for swallowing. Synonyms are *magoon* (India), *majun* (Turkey), and *madjun* (North Africa).

For *dawamesk* (or *dawamesc*) the hashish powder or flowering tops are simmered in butter or oil of almonds or sesame and strained. The oily extract containing most of the cannabinoids is flavored with cinnamon and cloves, musk, etc., and aphrodisiacs are often added. *Mapushari* is the term used if rose extract and powder are added. *Mosmok, mosjuk, teriyaki, banghia, malak, assyuni,* and *teridka* are names for related preparations. The following is the recipe for a confection of this type from Morocco.

| | |
|---|---|
| Almonds and walnuts | 1 kg |
| Cubeb, Nutmegs, Malaguetta pepper | 250 g |
| Datura seeds, Belladonna Berries | 50 g |
| Cannabis Tips, Honey | 1 kg |
| Butter | 500 g |

*Garawish* varies in that the ingredients are added to a well-cooked syrup, thickened with further heating and poured on an oiled surface to cool. In Algeria, barley sugar was used in its preparation.

Powdered hashish or flowering tops are sometimes added to *rahat lokum* (Turkish Delight) along with starch, sugar, water, nuts and essences of rose and orange. The hard, rectangular pieces are rolled in starch and sugar in the East, but the familiar candy of this name is sold in the West without the coating.

The stuffing in dates sometimes contains hashish. *Kiste,. kibarfi, misari,* and *kulfi* are prepared in India and occasionally elsewhere; and *briji, capsh, ikinji* and *zahra* are found in Syria and Palestine.

# 6

# Extraction of THC
# and Preparation of Hash Oil

## Sample Preparation

The extraction of the cannabinoids can be performed by itself,
or combined in a single operation with isomerization and preparation of hash oil. It is best to remove seeds and give them to a
friendly farmer; large stems should also be taken out, but neither
of these is really necessary. The material can be powdered in a
blender for somewhat faster extraction. Hashish should be
heated and crumbled up first. Marijuana should first be dried,
especially if you are working with fresh-picked plants. THC and
CBD will commonly be present in their acid form, which may
not be highly soluble in some solvents. For best results, convert
them to their nonacid forms by heating the marijuana or hashish for ten minutes at 120° F or five minutes at 200° F in an
oven. Research has shown that it is not possible to extract more
than 50% of the cannabinoids from fresh, undried material.
Three days at room temperature (circa 25° C) causes about a
70% weight loss (about 8% of the remaining weight is water),
and no further loss occurs unless the marijuana is heated.

## Solvents

A wide variety of organic solvents will work, but availability,
cost, toxicity and flammability will limit the choices. Research
has shown that chloroform is the best solvent; it extracts about
98% of the cannabinoids with one half hour of shaking. Light
petroleum ether extracts about 90%. But ethanol (grain alcohol)
is most often used. It is easier to obtain and extracts a high percentage as well. Ninety-five percent ethanol is hard to obtain,

but denatured 95% ethanol works just fine. Isopropyl alcohol (rubbing alcohol is 70% isopropanol) and methanol work, but the latter, especially industrial methanol, has rather toxic and explosive fumes. The alcohols extract undesirable water soluble substances such as chlorophylls and sugars, which you may wish to remove later by washing with water if you are making hash oil. (You can also do a water extraction prior to solvent extraction—David Hoye's "Double Wash Oil.") Common organic solvents such as benzene, chloroform and petroleum et1er will not extract the water soluble constituents of marijuana or hashish, and will yield a somewhat more potent oil as a result. However, their vapors are more flammable and they are harder to obtain. Methylene chloride (dichloromethane) works well. Unleaded gas, preferably without additives (white gas), paint thinner, or turpentine may work also, but undesirable odors or residues might remain. IT CANNOT BE TOO STRONGLY EMPHASIZED THAT ALL THESE SOLVENTS ARE FLAMMABLE AND DEVICES WHICH EMIT SPARKS OR FLAMES SUCH AS MOTORS OR PILOT LIGHTS ON APPLIANCES SHOULD NOT BE PRESENT. SMOKING IS HAZARDOUS. NONSPARKING MOTORS CAN BE OBTAINED. GOOD VENTILATION IS MANDATORY.

## TABLE 10

### Common Cannabinoid Solvents

| Name | Solvent Quality | Flammability | Toxicity | Availability |
|---|---|---|---|---|
| Chloroform | High | High | High | Low |
| Petroleum Ether | High | High | High | Medium |
| Benzene | High | High | High | Low |
| Ethanol | Medium | Medium | Low | High |
| Methanol | Medium | Medium | High | High |
| Isopropanol | Medium | Medium | Medium | High |
| Methylene Chloride (Dichloromethane) | High | None | Medium | Medium |

# Apparatus and Procedure

Those with lab apparatus can do the extraction and concentration in a standard refluxing setup (e.g., heating mantle for five liter flask with water cooled reflux head). The rest of us can manage with homemade devices such as those pictured. The water in the tub or bottom half of the double boiler heats up the solvent containing the marijuana. The warm solvent gradually extracts the cannabinoids, and some of it evaporates in the process. The solvent vapors condense on the ice-cooled lid and drop back down into the solvent containing the marijuana. This process of evaporating and recondensing solvent is called refluxing. Vapors do not escape into the air because of the seal formed by the plastic and rubber bands. If the ice melts (or in the one variety pictured, the cold water is not running fast enough), the pressure builds up and fumes escape around the edges of the plastic seal. The time of refluxing varies with the efficiency of the solvent. Chloroform or dichloromethane will probably not require more than ten minutes, while ethanol or isopropanol may need several hours for complete extraction. This may be tested roughly by removing, *carefully* drying, and smoking some of the grass. When extraction is complete, the device is cooled, the marijuana removed from the solvent and placed in the strainer, and the resealed apparatus again turned on. A few minutes of refluxing should suffice to wash most of the remaining cannabinoids from the marijuana. This second step will frequently be unnecessary since only a small amount of cannabinoids will be saved this way—though more will be saved if fresh solvent is used for this step.

After discarding the marijuana from the strainer or filtering it out of the solvent, the next step is to concentrate the solvent containing the cannabinoids. This is achieved by placing a pan or beaker above the strainer, resealing the apparatus and refluxing. The solvent now collects in the pan or beaker, resulting in the concentration of the cannabinoids in the inner pail or the top of the double boiler. When most of the solvent has collected in the pan or beaker, the apparatus can be cooled, opened and the pan or beaker removed, saving the essentially pure solvent for reuse. A portion of marijuana may be placed in the remain-

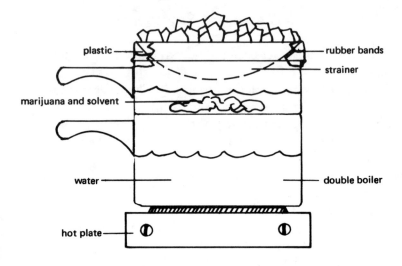

Fig. 15.  Design for extraction and isomerization apparatus

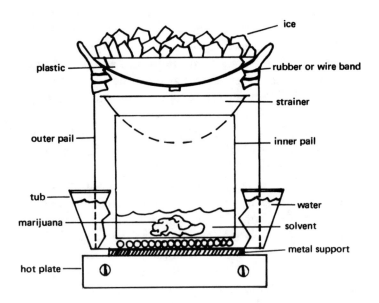

Fig. 16.  Design for extraction and isomerization apparatus

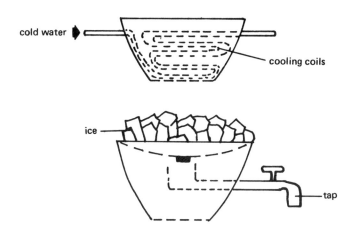

Fig. 17.  Alternative designs for the top portion of Figures 15 and 16

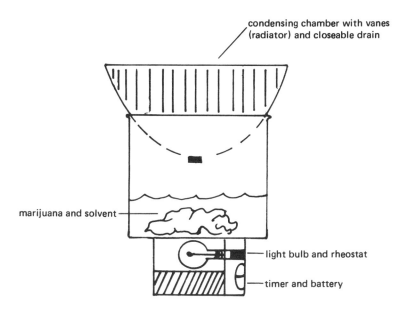

Fig. 18.  Air-cooled automatic battery-operated extractor-isomerizer

ing solvent, mixed thoroughly, and evaporation of the *small* amount of remaining solvent completed (good ventilation). If you use an ounce of marijuana for this and you used a pound for the extraction, the ounce should wind up roughly 16 times stronger. If you wish to make hash oil instead, add a small amount of water to the remaining solvent and continue evaporation until all the water has disappeared, since all the remaining solvent will disappear first. This can also be done by placing the inner pail or top of the double boiler in a cooking oil or mineral oil bath and heating to about 230° F until all the water evaporates. Sometimes a gummy residue rather than an oil may be obtained. It should still be possible to obtain an oil by using the following purification methods. Apparatus for large scale extraction is described in *Lloydia 33*:453 (1970) and *Cannabis Alchemy* (Level Press, 1973).

If heating is gentle, and the surface area in contact with the vapors is large, neither ice nor running cold water will be necessary for condensation. The principle involved is the same as that of the air-cooled radiator in cars. Air cooling is more likely to succeed in a cool room, out of doors, or with a fan creating an air flow over the top of the apparatus. With air cooling, it is necessary to be extra careful that no vapors are escaping into the room.

The heating coil (hotplate) can be replaced by a lightbulb and the current regulated with a rheostat for a gentle, easily controlled heat source. An electrical timer would make the operation automatic and the whole device could be battery powered for use in areas without electricity or running water. Air cooling, lightbulb heating and a timer are employed in the isomerizer discussed in the next chapter.

## Purification

This can be done with various solvents, but alcohols should not be used since the materials one wishes to eliminate from the oil are also soluble in the alcohol. Dissolve the oily residue from the extraction in three to six times its volume of benzene, gasoline, petroleum, or ether, and add an equal volume of water. Shake in a large bottle or separatory funnel and carefully release the pressure every few shakes. Let stand for a few minutes to half an hour and separate the top solvent layer containing the cannabinoids from the lower water layer and the middle emulsion layer. The water plus emulsion layers can be shaken with further fresh solvent to remove the last traces of cannabinoids. Extraction is complete when the solvent is clear. Place the combined solvent extracts in the inner pail or top of the double boiler, place a pan or beaker above the strainer as before, seal the apparatus with the plastic and rubber bands and place ice in the lid as before. Reflux until almost all the solvent has been collected in the beaker, then open the apparatus and evaporate the remaining solvent as before. If you desire to remove the colored impurities from the oil, add activated charcoal equal to about one third to one half the weight or volume of the solvent containing the dissolved oil, mix well and filter. Evaporate the solvent as usual. This oil should contain roughly ten times the concentration of cannabinoids present in the original marijuana. Artificial hashish can be made by adding oil to blenderized marijuana in a ratio of from 10 to 50% oil, kneading and drying.

## Special Extraction Apparatus

An apparatus which allows for continuous extraction and removal of hash oil is depicted in figure 18. The oil is occasionally tapped from the lower container and from time to time the device must be cooled and the marijuana or hashish in the upper container changed. Many variations are possible; several are noted in the following comments from the DEA.

## The DEA Comments on Hash Oil

The following comments were made by the DEA (Drug Enforcement Administration) in 1973:

> There are many ways to produce hashish oil, but the basic principle used by most clandestine operators is similar to that of percolating coffee. A basket filled with ground or chopped up marijuana

Fig. 19. Apparatus for continuous extraction of hash oil. Thin tubing brings the mixture of cannabinoids in solvent from the first pressure cooker in the background through the top of the second cooker which is painted black to absorb heat. Heat lamps are used to evaporate the solvent which rises through the insulated plastic pipe. The DEA stated that this apparatus produced 2.5 quarts of oil from about 82 pounds of marijuana in one hour. The time is unquestionably too short, but if the other figures are correct and grass with 1% THC content was used, the oil would contain about 20% THC. (Reprinted from *Drug Enforcement,* 1973.)

Fig. 20. Another view of the second cooker shows the tube through which the final product is drained into jars. (Reprinted from *Drug Enforcement,* 1973.)

plant is suspended inside a larger container, at the bottom of which is contained a solvent, such as alcohol, hexane, chloroform or petroleum ether. Copper tubing or similar material is arranged at the top through which cold water circulates. The solvent is heated and the vapors rise to the top where they condense, then fall into the basket of marijuana. As the solvent seeps through the plant material, the THC and other soluble chemicals are dissolved, and the solution drops back to the bottom of the container. Continued heating causes the process to occur over and over again. The solution becomes increasingly stronger until the plant material is exhausted of its THC. Sometimes new material is added and the same solvent reheated, yielding an even more potent solution. Only simple equipment is required. One laboratory used a 55-gallon drum in which was supported a smaller, perforated drum. Copper tubing, attached to a wooden lid, was connected to a cold water supply. Another laboratory

used more elaborate equipment with cooling coils
and reflux column 'potted' in plastic.

One seizure revealed a veritable 'Rube Gold-
berg' machine consisting of a boiler, a heat exchang-
er, a vacuum assembly and other components (with
parts list, instructions and assembly methods) for a
sophisticated hashish oil apparatus which was sched-
uled to be shipped to the Middle East.

Hashish laboratories have been seized in the
middle and western United States, Mexico, and
South America. Hashish oil itself has been found in
several parts of the United States, in Central and
South America, and in Europe. Most of the hashish
oil that has been confiscated originated in India or
Afghanistan and was shipped via commercial freight
directly to the United States or Canada for forward-
ing. Thus far the senders and laboratory operators
have usually been U.S. citizens.

The high THC content of hashish oil presents
serious problems to all concerned—the law enforcement officer, the scientist, and the user. For the
law enforcement officer, the shipment of hashish
oil complicates further an already complex problem. Instead of searching for large, fairly bulky
packages of hashish or marijuana, the officer must
search for smaller, more easily hidden liquid containers. The material can be dissolved in liquor, af-
tershave lotion, perfume, or commercial solvents.
It may be packaged in heat sealed plastic bags and
placed on the bottoms of pickle barrels, fuel tanks
of planes, boats or cars. Small vials of the oil can be
concealed in fountain pens or jewelry.

Meanwhile, the scientist faces the urgent task
of evaluating the effects of hashish oil with a THC
potency that may be as high as 90 percent.

The DEA also thinks that users face health hazards from
hash oil, and, while this is unquestionably true for persons who
use large amounts, the only hazard for most users will be the
law enforcement officers.

## TABLE 11

## THC Content of Hash Oil

| YEAR | SUPPOSED ORIGIN | % THC |
|------|-----------------|-------|
| Early 1973 | Afghanistan | 11.0 |
| | Afghanistan | 29.0 |
| | Afghanistan | 17.0 |
| | Colombia | 0.3 |
| | Colombia | 12.0 |
| | Colombia | 17.0 |
| | Morocco | 12.0 |
| | Nepal | 10.0 |
| | USA | 6.0 |
| | USA | 8.0 |
| | USA | 20.0 |
| | USA | 21.0 |
| | USA | 34.0 |
| Late 1973 | Afghanistan | 13.0 |
| | Afghanistan | 20.0 |
| | Morocco | 20.0 |
| | Nepal | 3.0 |
| | Nepal | 9.0 |
| | USA | 7.0 |
| | USA | 8.0 |
| | USA | 12.0 |
| | USA | 16.0 |
| | USA | 17.0 |
| | USA | 18.0 |
| | USA (Iowa) | 0.6 |
| 1974 | Afghanistan | 0.6 |
| | Afghanistan | 8.0 |
| | Afghanistan | 13.0 |

| YEAR | SUPPOSED ORIGIN | % THC |
|------|-----------------|-------|
| 1974 | Lebanon | 5.0 |
|  | Netherlands | 11.0 |
|  | USA | 11.0 |
|  | USA | 12.0 |
|  | USA | 16.0 |
|  | USA | 16.0 |
|  | USA (California) | 19.0 |
|  | USA (California) | 20.0 |
|  | USA (California | 31.0 |
|  | USA (Iowa) | 1.3 |
|  | USA (Kentucky) | 18.0 |

SOURCE: "Pharmchem Reports 1973-1974," Pharmchem Research Foundation, Palo Alto, California

## THC Content of Hash Oil

As can be seen from table 11, the THC content of hash oil varies tremendously. This is only to be expected, since the manufacturers use a random assortment of marijuana and preparation techniques. Although CBD contents of hash oil have seldom been reported, they may tend to be somewhat higher in marijuana, since poorer quality marijuana may be used for oil preparation. On the other hand, since isomerization is so simple, as time passes, one may expect to find more and more oil that has been isomerized and which contains almost entirely THC. Much of the oil is being produced abroad; the Afghani government seized some 76 kg of oil in the period from July, 1973 through November, 1974. The oil available on the U.S. West Coast in 1974 averaged about 15% THC. Dealers sometimes cut hash oil with other oils, which means that the original hash oil may have averaged much higher. The ratio of THC to CBD should be identical to that of the marijuana used in preparing the oil unless the isomerization of CBD to THC, described in the next section, has been carried out. Thus, one oil prepared from Iowa grass had 1.3% THC and 31% CBD, and would be useless for anything except isomerization.

# 7

# Isomerization

## Principles

The final step in tetrahydrocannabinol biosynthesis in the living plant is the dehydration of CBD to THC. This is catalyzed by a specific enzyme coded for by a single gene. In principle, it should be a simple matter to extract the cannabinoids using a wide variety or organic solvents and to perform dehydration on the mixture, converting any CBD present into THC. In practice, this is, in fact, extremely easy to do since merely refluxing (heating with an apparatus for returning the cooled vapor to the reaction mixture) the organic extract with a small amount of an acid such as HCl or sulfuric acid is sufficient to isomerize the CBD to THC in a few minutes. The acid provides hydrogen ions (protons) which catalyze (speed up) the dehydration of CBD to THC. Look at figure 1 where it is clear that a hydrogen atom has been transferred from an oxygen atom (CBD) to a carbon atom (THC).

## Procedure

The general procedure and apparatus are identical to those already described for the extraction. The isomerization of CBD to THC is accomplished by refluxing with a small quantity of organic or inorganic acid. If alcohol is being used, add about 2 ml of 1 normal HCl (prepared by adding 120 g concentrated HCl slowly to 900 ml water) or 2 ml of 1 normal sulfuric acid (prepared by adding 30 ml concentrated sulfuric acid slowly to 1 liter of water) for each 200 ml solvent (roughly the amount needed for 100 g of marijuana). If benzene or petroleum ether or other relatively nonpolar solvent (most common ones other than alcohols) are being used, 100 mg paratoluenesulfonic acid or 684 mg (0.006 moles) trifluoroacetic acid are used instead of the HCl or sulfuric acid. Roughly four times as much acid can be used if hashish is being isomerized. The object is to have about 1 g of CBD in 100 ml solvent that is 0.005 molar (about 0.05%) in acid content.

Assemble the apparatus described; add the marijuana, hashish or hash oil; the solvent and the acid; seal and reflux (i.e., heat gently) for about one hour. You can expect about 90% of the CBD to isomerize to $\Delta^1$ THC if an organic solvent such as benzene or petroleum ether is used, but only about 60% yield of $\Delta^1$ and $\Delta^6$ THC's with other products (e.g., ethoxyhexahydrocannibinols) if ethanol or another alcohol is used. If the cannabinoids have already been extracted; i.e., if you have hash oil, you may simply dissolve the oil in solvent and heat with acid to get isomerization. For example, a saturated solution of paratoluenesulfonic acid in methylene chloride heated at 80° F for 45 minutes gives about 90% yield of THC. As the reaction times are increased, more $\Delta^1$ THC will isomerize to $\Delta^6$ THC, but since the two have nearly the same activity, this does not matter. For oil, use about 5 ml oil per 100 ml solvent.

The solvent may now be removed, leaving the isomerized cannabinoids behind as an oily residue (deposited on the marijuana if this is left in). Solvent removal is accomplished exactly as described in the extraction section. Although the amount of acid used is small, you may wish to neutralize it with a small quantity of base, such as baking soda, prior to evaporation of solvent. Also, if you have used alcohol for isomerization (or extraction), you may shake the large volumes of alcohol containing the cannabinoids with benzene, petroleum ether, or other nonpolar solvents. The cannabinoids are much more soluble in the latter, and the smaller volume is easier to evaporate. Again, if the latter solvents are used, it is good to wash them with water several times (i.e., shake with an equal volume of water and discard the water) before evaporation to rid them of the undesirable water soluble substances, even if the marijuana has been water-extracted prior to isomerization (David Hoye's "Double Wash" technique).

# Automation

The area of extraction and isomerization has been pioneered by David Hoye, inventor of the world's first automated isomerizer. At $179 this machine may seem over-priced, but it has the advantage of being significantly safer than home-built apparati. One can easily imagine this machine becoming a common item in the American kitchen along with the toaster and electric blender. However, claims that it will double the potency of any marijuana without weight loss are obviously untrue. This would require about twice as much CBD as THC being present, a very rare situation with commercial marijuana.

# Deciding When to Isomerize

Isomerization is desirable only when the marijuana has significant quantities of CBD. Thus, good-quality marijuana such as that from Mexico, Colombia, or Southeast Asia, will usually not be suitable for isomerization, though it can be extracted and concentrated. However, some strains from these areas contain considerable CBD even when their THC content is high. Wild marijuana from northern latitudes, or that cultivated for fiber in such areas as the U.S., Europe, or Turkey, will usually have considerable CBD. It should be kept in mind that low THC does not necessarily mean high CBD. Some strains are extremely low in all types of cannabinoids. A study of wild stands in Illinois showed THC varying from almost none to 2.3% and CBD from almost none to 7.1%. The only sensible thing to do is to first analyze for CBD content. Various labs will do this, though if you desire a quantitative analysis, you must first obtain from them a controlled drugs transfer form (this idiocy has been forced on them by the DEA). You can also assay for CBD yourself by performing the extremely simple Beam test for CBD discussed in the testing section. The only problem lies in the need for a standard with a known CBD content, though this need may be circumvented if someone markets a well standardized test with a color chart (the Beam test gives a purple color with CBD).

# 8

# Testing for THC and CBD Content

## Colorimetry

There are color tests which are relatively specific for marijuana, but for present purposes we want a rapid, simple, roughly quantitative test which differentiates between CBD and THC. Ammoniacal silver nitrate gives a green color with CBD and no color with THC or CBN, but the Beam test likewise reacts only with CBD and is simpler. It is desirable to first dry the marijuana in an oven at 200° F for five minutes. Add 1 g of dry marijuana, preferably finely powdered, to 10 ml petroleum ether or other organic solvent, shake and let stand ten minutes. Evaporate 0.2 ml of the filtered extract in a white porcelain dish, spot plate, or test tube. (Use gentle heat from hotplate or water bath.) Add four drops 5% potassium hydroxide in ethanol (5 g solid KOH in 95 ml of 95% ethanol) to the residue and wait five minutes for the violet color to appear. Samples with known CBD content can be tested simultaneously to give a standard curve, if a colorimeter is available; if not, rough quantitation can be done by comparing the colors by eye. Colored papers or pencils can be used to match the color of known CBD contents, and these colors can subsequently be used to roughly quantitate unknown samples. Extracting the marijuana with water prior to performing the Beam test may help to quantitate it.

At the present time there seems to be no good color test which reacts only with THC. However, if the Beam test is first run and shows the presence of relatively little CBD, many different tests can then be applied to the marijuana to roughly quantitate the THC content by first subtracting the value of the

Beam test. One of the easiest of these is the Duquenois test. Prepare an extract as above and evaporate it to dryness. Add four
drops Duquenois reagent (0.4 g vanillin, five drops acetaldehyde
in 20 ml 95% ethanol), then eight drops concentrated HCl, mix
and let stand ten minutes. The violet color can be compared
against standards of known THC content as above. If the color
is too intense, use less sample or less extract and vice versa.

Samples can be sent to labs for quantitative analyses, but
you will have to go through some paperwork and hassles; so you
may prefer to roughly quantitate the test by analyzing marijuana you have already smoked.

Many tests give different colors with CBD, CBN and THC,
and these might be used to measure CBD and THC simultaneously, especially if a colorimeter is available.[1]

## Fluorimetry

Some recent experiments hold out hope for measuring THC by
flourescence techniques. THC gives an intense greenish-yellow
color under a black light with the following reaction, while CBN
gives a weak reaction and CBD does not react. Extract 1 g of dry
(preferably heated for 5 minutes at 200° F) marijuana for two
minutes with 5 ml petroleum ether, benzene, chloroform, or
similar solvent. Filter, evaporate the solvent on a boiling water
bath to dryness and add 0.5 ml concentrated sulfuric acid. Cover
tube and mix the acid with the residue, then heat carefully for
ten seconds on a boiling water bath and cool. Carefully add
10 ml 20% ammonium hydroxide, mix and examine under
black light. It may be possible to do the reaction directly on the
marijuana without first extracting with a solvent, but it may
need to be filtered before examining in black light. Again, standard marijuana with known THC concentrations will be needed,
but a series of fluorescent standards can be prepared. Those with
a fluorimeter available can probably dispense with standards
once they standardize the test on their machine. Those with a
machine available may also make use of the fact that heating
the residue of the marijuana extract for 15 minutes at 230° F
and redissolving in solvent gives fluorescence emission peaks at

420 nm for THC and 440 nm for CBD and CBN. If fluorescence is too intense in any test, use less marijuana for extraction or dilute solvent.[2] This test is very experimental and will probably be hard to adapt to home use. It is given here only to stimulate research.

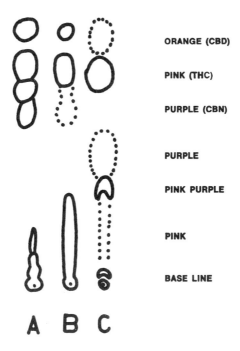

ORANGE (CBD)

PINK (THC)

PURPLE (CBN)

PURPLE

PINK PURPLE

PINK

BASE LINE

A  B  C

Fig. 21.  Thin layer chromatogram of marijuana extract. *A* is from marijuana; *B* is from hashish; and *C* is from the hand of a marijuana smoker. Small spots of the extracts are placed on the base line, the solvent rises by capillary action from the bottom to the top carrying the compounds with it at varying rates. After drying, the plate is sprayed with a color-developing reagent and the spots identified by comparing with standards.

## Chromatography

Chromatography on thin layers of silica gel or alumina is a standard technique for identifying and separating marijuana constituents. Marijuana is extracted with solvent as described above, and a small amount is spotted with a capillary tube or micropipette on one end of the plate. The plate is then placed vertically in a small amount of solvent. The solvent is drawn to the other end by capillary action, which carries the cannabinoids present in the extract varying distances up the plate. The plate is then dried and sprayed with a dye which develops different colors with the various cannabinoids. The procedure is easier than it sounds, and with a little practice could be done at home; it will still require known standards to give very roughly quantitative results. Some of the dyes originally used as spray reagents are now being used in field tests for marijuana. They could easily be used to give at least rough quantitative results.[3]

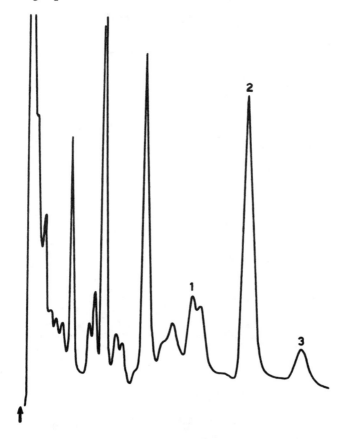

Fig. 22.  Gas chromatogram of an extract of marijuana. 1 is CBD; 2 is $\Delta^1$-THC; 3 is CBN. In this procedure a small amount of the liquid extract is injected into a long heated coil through which gas passes. The thousands of compounds leave the column at different times and are detected and displayed as a series of irregular peaks seen above. Injection of known standards allows identification of the peaks.

# Appendix
## Chemical Syntheses

### JOURNAL ABBREVIATIONS

| | |
|---|---|
| ACS | Acta Chemica Scandinavica |
| AP | Archiv der Pharmazie |
| BCSJ | Bulletin of the Chemical Society of Japan |
| BER | Berichte der Deutsche Chemische Gesellschaft |
| BSC | Bulletin de la Societe Chimique de France |
| CA | Chemical Abstracts |
| CCCC | Collection of Czechoslovakian Chemical Communications |
| CJC | Canadian Journal of Chemistry |
| CPB | Chemical and Pharmaceutical Bulletin |
| CT | Chimie Therapeutique (Chimica Therapeutica) |
| GCI | Gazzetta Chimica Italiana |
| HCA | Helvetica Chimica Acta |
| JACS | Journal of the American Chemical Society |
| JBC | Journal of Biological Chemistry |
| JCS | Journal of the Chemical Society |
| JGC | Journal of General Chemistry (English translation of Zhurnal Obschei Kimii) |
| JHC | Journal of Heterocyclic Chemistry |
| JMC | Journal of Medicinal Chemistry |
| JOC | Journal of Organic Chemistry |
| JPS | Journal of Pharmaceutical Science |
| LAC | Leibigs Annalen der Chemie |
| MON | Monatshefte fur Chemie |
| REC | Recueil Travaux Chemiques |
| TET | Tetrahedron |
| TL | Tetrahedron Letters |

## CHEMICAL HINTS

Much useful information can be found in any lab text in organic chemistry such as that of Wiberg.

### Drying

Shake the solution with an anhydrous salt such as $MgSO_4$, $Na_2SO_4$, etc. and filter out the salt. Solids can be dried by spreading on a filter paper at room temperature or drying in an oven at low heat.

### Solvents

All solvents should be anhydrous unless otherwise specified. This can sometimes be done by drying as above and is to be attended to especially in the case of ethanol which is available in 95% or 100% (100% takes up water from the air very rapidly).

### Joints

Whenever apparatus with ground glass joints is used, Dow silicone grease provides excellent lubrication and airtight seal.

### Petroleum Ether

This usually refers to the light boiling fraction (60°-80° C) of petroleum ether which must not be confused with "ether," which refers to diethyl ether.

### Vacuum Evaporation

This requires a heavy-walled flask. Ordinary lab vacuums are about 15mm Hg. A simple water-forced suction vacuum requires only a water source to produce a vacuum of about 25mm Hg, which is satisfactory for most purposes. Evaporation causes the temperature to drop which slows evaporation. Running a stream of warm water over the flask or putting it in a warm water bath avoids this. To avoid difficulties in getting residues out of the

Fig. 23. Vacuum exsiccator

bottom of the flask, it is useful to do the evaporation in a vacuum exsiccator shaped as shown or in a flat dish in the exsiccator. Whenever a forced water vacuum is used, it is wise to place a water trap between the vacuum and the solvent being evaporated to prevent water from entering when the pressure fluctuates.

*Stirring*
This can be done in the old way with a stirring propeller entering through one of the necks of the flask, attached to a nonsparking motor. It is easier to sit the flask on a magnetic stirrer, and drop a magnetic stirring bar (preferably Teflon coated and egg shaped for round-bottom flask) in the solution.

*Heating and Refluxing*
Do not smoke or have any flames (such as a pilot light on gas appliances) around when using organic solvents, especially ether. Bunsen or other types of gas burners are generally outmoded. Much better are electric heating mantles available for each size of round-bottom flask. Put a rheostat in the circuit to regulate the temperature of the mantle. For refluxing, adjust the rheostat so that the vapor level in the water-cooled condenser is about a quarter of the way up the condenser. Heating plates or combination heating plate-magnetic stirrer is also useful.

*Ventilation*
If a lab hood is not available, some forced air ventilation such as a large fan near a window is advisable, especially if ether is used.

*Lithium Aluminum Hydride*
Lithium aluminum hydride is expensive and often difficult to obtain. It can be synthesized [JACS *69*,1197(1947)], but this is rather tricky. Its use can usually be circumvented by using a different reducing method or a different synthetic route.

*Safety*
An explosion shield, asbestos gloves, face mask and tongs are desirable.

*A Substitute for Raney-Nickel,* JACS *85*,1004(1963)
5 mMoles Ni acetate in 50 ml water in 125 ml erlenmeyer flask;

connect as below to Hg pressure outlet. Flush with $N_2$, stir and add over 30 seconds with the syringe, 10 ml 1M $NaBH_4$ in water. After hydrogen evolution ceases, add 5 ml more of $NaBH_4$. Decant the aqueous phase, wash solid with 2X50 ml ethanol to get the Ni-boride catalyst as a black, granular solid. Hydrogenation can then be done as described below at room temperature and atmospheric pressure.

*A Highly Active Raney-Nickel Catalyst*, JOC 26,1625(1961)
Add with stirring, in small portions over one-half hour, 40g 50% Raney-Ni to 600 ml 10% NaOH in a 1L three-neck flask and continue stirring one hour. Let the Ni settle and decant the solution. Wash residue with 5X200 ml water, 5X50 ml ethanol, always keeping the Ni covered with liquid. Store under ethanol in refrigerator. Hydrogenation with this catalyst can be carried out in a low pressure Parr bottle (e.g., 30-80 ml ethanol, 5-10g Ni suspension, 1-2 ml 20% NaOH, 40°-50° and 40-60 PSI $H_2$).

## A New Method for Hydrogenating at Room Temperature and Atmospheric Pressure

*Method 1: External Generation of Hydrogen*
    JACS 75,215(1953)
This method reduces the solvent volume in the reducing flask for large-scale work. Add 1M $NaBH_4$ in water to an aqueous HCl or acetic acid solution containing a little $CoCl_2$, if necessary for a rapid rate.

*Method 2: Internal Generation of Hydrogen*
    JACS 84,1494-5,2827-30(1962)
Three-necked flask fitted with a graduated dropping funnel or a 50 ml burette, an inlet port fitted with a rubber serum cap, and an Hg manometer which allows gas to escape when the pressure exceeds about 25 mm above atmospheric pressure. At room temperature (25° C water bath) with stirring, add 1 ml 0.2M chloroplatinic acid (commercial 10% is about 0.2M) to 40 ml ethanol and lg decolorizing carbon (e.g., Darco KB—may omit this but the reaction is slower). Flush with $N_2$ if possible and add 5 ml 1M $NaBH_4$ (prepared from 3.8g $NaBH_4$, 95 ml ethanol, 5 ml 2N NaOH) rapidly to a vigorously stirred solution (black precipitate forms). After about one minute inject about 4 ml

concentrated HCl or glacial acetic acid to initiate hydrogen generation. Then inject about 0.02M of the unsaturated compound. Add $NaBH_4$ dropwise so that flask pressure remains about atmospheric pressure. Reaction is over when uptake ceases. $NaBH_4$ addition can be made automatic by putting a syringe full of it in an Hg-filled tube (about 15mm Hg, with holes so that as the pressure drops, more solution enters). This apparatus is available from Delmar Scientific Labs. Can also use $PtCl_2$, $PtCl_4$, Ni, Rhodium, $PtO_2$, platinum-carbon catalyst, palladium-carbon catalyst in place of chloroplatinic acid, but the last three are poor. Other salts can be used in place of the chlorides.

Note that the above procedures permit hydrogenation without the use of hydrogen tanks or special hydrogenation apparatus (Parr bottles, etc.).

Other references on the use of boron compounds for reduction: Org. Rxns. *13*,28(1963); JACS *86*,3566(1964); JOC *28*, 3261(1963); JCS 371(1962).

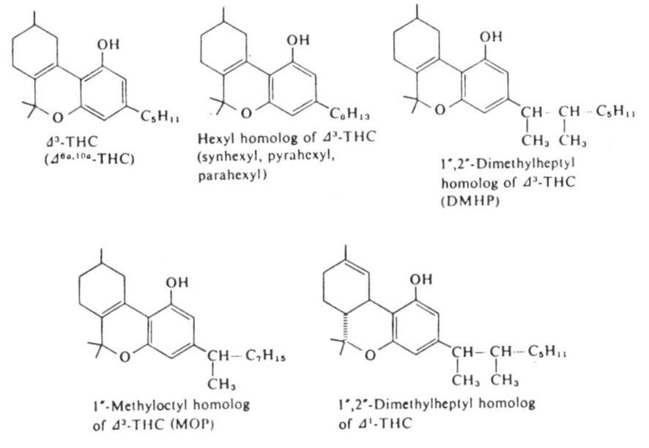

Fig. 24. Some widely tested synthetic cannabinoids

## IS IT LEGAL?

The $\Delta^1$ and $\Delta^{1(6)}$ THC's with the n-pentyl in the 5' position (obtained by using olivetol in the syntheses) are naturally occurring and hence illegal, but the $\Delta^3$ THC's and the numerous isomers, homologs and analogs of the $\Delta^1$ and $\Delta^{1(6)}$ compounds are probably legal.

Apparently, recent federal legislation outlaws delta-1, delta-1(6), delta-3,4-THC's, both cis and trans and D and L and compounds. This still leaves hundreds of legal cannabinoids.

## STRUCTURE-ACTIVITY RELATIONSHIPS

THC refers to tetrahydrocannabinol, and $\Delta$ refers to the position of the double bond. Various numbering systems are used, so the following equivalences should be noted: $\Delta^1$ THC = $\Delta^1$ 3,4-trans-THC = $\Delta^9$ THC and $\Delta^6$ THC = $\Delta^{1\,(6)}$ THC = $\Delta^8$ THC = $\Delta^6$-3, 4-trans-THC.

Little careful human testing has been done, so data given here and elsewhere on the relative psychedelic activity of various cannabinoids is often only a rough guess. $\Delta^1$ THC and $\Delta^6$ THC have about the same activity which is about five times that of $\Delta^3$ THC. Cannabidiol, cannabidiolic acid, cannabinol, cannabigerol and cannabichromene all have very little or no activity. Only the $\ell$ (-) isomer of THC seems to be active. When the n-pentyl at the 5' position is replaced by 1,2-dimethylheptyl, potency and duration of action increases about five times, giving the most active THC analog yet tested.

It should be noted that recent testing has indicated that a 1,1-dimethylheptyl or 1-methyloctyl and probably similar side chains give THC's of equal or greater activity than the 1,2-dimethylheptyl cpd. However, the difficulty of synthesizing these compounds plus their very long action (up to several days or more) makes it doubtful whether they deserve all the interest they have generated among psychedelic enthusiasts. More concern should be devoted to the shorter side chains, since they would presumably allow one to get very stoned but to be straight again within a few hours, thus allowing the drug to be more easily manipulated.

Substituting N, O, or S atoms at various places or saturating the double bond to produce hexahydrocannabinol probably retains activity. [See *CA* 74,125667(1971) for S analogs.] Alkoxy side chains at 5' retain activity. Unsaturated side chains are as active as saturated ones. Ether moieties at the 5' position, but not as the 3', retain activity. Activity is retained if an additional alkyl is placed at 4' but lost if placed at 6'. Activity is greatly decreased or lost if the H at the 4' or 6' positions is replaced by carboxyl, carbomethoxyl, acetyl or acetoxyl; if the hydroxyl is replaced by H; if the OH is at 5' and the side chain at 4'. Methyl and/or ethyl at 1 and 5 retains activity, as does removal of the methyl at 1. An hydroxyl in the side chain is active, but not on the first carbon of the side chain. Esterifying the OH retains activity, but etherifying eliminates activity.

THC can be synthesized via cannabigerol and cannabichromene in low yield [TET $24$,4830(1968), TL 5349,5353(1969), Proc. Chem. Soc. 82,(1964)]. For several moderately difficult routes leading to $\Delta^{1(6)}$ THC via cannabinol in about 10% yield, see LAC $685$,126(1965). For a synthesis of $\Delta^{1(6)}$ THC from cinnamyl derivatives and isoprene see JACS $89$,4551(1967). A rather difficult synthesis of $\Delta^1$ and $\Delta^{1(6)}$ THC is given in JACS $89$,5934(1967). For a variety of THC analogs of unknown activity see BSC 1374, 1384(1968); JCS 952(1949); JACS $63$, 1971,1977,2766(1941), $64$,694,2031,2653(1942), $67$,1534 (1945), $70$,662(1948), $71$,1624(1949), $82$,5198(1960); CA $75$,48910(1971); TL 3405(1967); JMC $11$,377(1968); CT 2, 167(1967); CA $76$,126783(1972).

Since 0 or 1 and perhaps 2 double bonds anywhere in the lefthand ring above, as well as changes in the size and position of the alkyl groups will probably all produce compounds with THC activity, many compounds similar to menthadieneol, menthatriene, verbenol, epoxycarene, pulegone and 4-carbethoxy-1-Me-3-cyclohexanone can be used in the methods below to get active THC analogs (e.g., isopiperitinol will work [TL 945 (1972)]). Also, 5-chlororesorcinol and 5-methylresorcinol (orcinol) have been shown to give weakly active THC's [see CA $76$,33946(1972), US Patent 3,028,410(1962), and TET $23$, 3435(1967) for syntheses of orcinol and related compounds]. Unfortunately, recent data indicate that orcinol gives a THC with very low activity. It appears that delta-5 and delta-7 THC have very little activity. If the methyl groups at carbon 8 in THC are changed to longer alkyl groups, the activity decreases, but the replacement of the alkyl groups by hydrogen or other groups has not been carried out. Open chain analogs also have activity [see CT $2$,167(1967)].

For new information on the structure-activity relationships of cannabinoids see JMC $16$,1200(1973), Arzneim, Forsch $22$, 1995(1972), and Chem. Revs. $76$,75(1976).

For THC analogs see JMC $19$,445-71,549-53(1976); Eur. JMC $10$,79(1975); Phytochem. $14$,213(1975); CA $82$,57564, 170672-3(1975); Diss. Abst. $34B$,1442(1973); J. Labelled Cpds.

11,551(1975); Compt. Rend. Acad. Sci. *281C*,197(1975).

For THC in one step from chrysanthenol see Experientia *31*,16(1975).

The following gives the synthesis of a water soluble THC derivative which is equipotent with THC and perhaps more rapidly acting (see Science *177*,442(1972)). Stir equimolar amounts of THC, dicyclohexylcarbodiimide and gamma-morpholinobutyric acid hydrochloride (or gamma-piperidinobutyric acid hydrochloride) [JACS *83*,2891(1961)] in methylene chloride at room temperature for 16 hours and filter, evaporate in vacuum (can triturate with ether and filter). The cost of synthetic THC will vary greatly depending on many factors, but high quality grass can probably be produced for under $20 a kilo.

For good reviews of marijuana chemistry see Prog. Chem. Natural Prod. *25*,175(1967), Science *168*,1159(1970), C. Joyce and J. Curry (Eds.), *Botany and Chemistry of Cannabis* (1970), JACS *93*,217(1971), JPS *60*,1433(1971), Ann. N.Y. Acad. Sci. *191*(1971), Prog. Org. Chem. *8*,78(1973), Marijuana-R. Mechoulam (Ed.) (1973), and Chemical Reviews *76*,75(1976).

Only the first three methods below give the natural ℓ (-) isomer of THC. The other methods give the racemic product and consequently their yields of active THC are actually one-half that indicated.

## SYNTHESES OF THC AND ANALOGS

ℓ(-)-$\Delta^{1\,(6)}$ *THC* HCA *52*,1123(1969), cf. JACS *96*,5860(1974).

### Method 1

This method gives about 50% yield for THC and about 90% for the 1',1'-dimethylpentyl analog.

Olivetol 4.74 g (or equimolar amount of analog), 4.03 g (+) cis or trans p-methadien (2,8)-ol-1 (the racemic compound can be used but yield will be one-half), 0.8 g p-toluenesulfonic acid in 250 ml benzene; reflux two hours (or use 0.004 Moles trifluoroacetic acid and reflux five hours). Cool, add ether, wash with $NaHCO_3$ and dry, evaporate in vacuum to get about 9 g of mixture (can chromatograph on 350 g silica gel- benzene elutes the THC; benzene: ether 98:2 elutes an inactive product; then benzene: ether 1:1 elutes unreacted olivetol; evaporate in vacuum to recover olivetol).

## Method 2

Dissolve the olivetol or analog and p-menthadienol or p-methatriene (1,5,8) in 8 ml liquid $SO_2$ in a bomb and fuse 70 hours at room temperature. Proceed as above to get about 20% yield.

$\ell(-)-\Delta^{1\,(6)}$ *THC* JACS *89*,4552(1967), JCS (C) 579(1971), cf. Diss. Abst. *35B*,3843(1974), and Phytochemistry 14,213(1975).

Convert (-) alpha-pinene to (-) verbenol (see precursors section). Add 1M (-) verbenol (racemic verbenol will give one-half yield), 1M olivetol or analog with methylene chloride as solvent. Add $BF_3$ etherate and let stand at room temperature one-half hour to get approximately 35% yield after evaporating in vacuum or purifying as above to recover unreacted olivetol. Solvent and catalyst used in method 1 above will probably also work. Either cis or trans verbenol can be used. The JCS paper adds 1g $BF_3$-etherate to a solution of 1g olivetol and 1.1g verbenol in 200 ml methylene chloride and let stand two hours at room temperature. JACS *94*,6164(1972) recommends two hours at -10° C, then one-half hour at room temperature and the use of cis rather than trans verbenol (the latter gradually decomposes at room temperature). The reaction is also carried out under nitrogen, using twice as much verbenol as olivetol, 0.85ml $BF_3$ etherate and 85 ml methylene chloride/g verbenol (both freshly distilled over calcium hydride) to give ca. 50% yield. See also JACS *94*,6159(1972) for the use of citral and Arzneim. Forsch. *22*,1995(1972) for use of p-TSA.

In the synthesis of THC with verbenol, the cis isomer is preferable to the trans since the latter decomposes at room temperature. Pinene or carvone give active THC's [JMC *17*,287(74)].

$\ell(-)$-$\Delta^1$ *and* $\Delta^{1\,(6)}$ *THC* JACS 92,6061(1970), U.S. Patent 3,734,930

1M (+)-trans-2-carene oxide (2-epoxycarene), 1M olivetol or analog, 0.05 M p-toluenesulfonic acid in 10L benzene; reflux two hours and evaporate in vacuum (or can separate the unreacted olivetol as above) to get about 30% yield THC. Olivetol can also be separated as described below. For synthesis of 2-epoxycarene ($\Delta^4$ carene oxide) from $\Delta^4$ carene (preparation given later) see p-methadieneol preparation (method 2). 3-carene oxide gives 20% yield of $\Delta^{1\,(6)}$ THC.

$\Delta^3$ *THC* JACS 63,2211(1941)

1M pulegone, 1M olivetol or analog, 0.3 M $POCl_3$; reflux four hours in 1 L benzene and evaporate in vacuum or pour into excess saturated $NaHCO_3$ and extract with dilute NaOH to recover unreacted olivetol. Dry, and evaporate in vacuum the benzene layer to get the THC.

$\Delta^{1\,(6)}$ *THC from Cannabidiol* HCA 52,1123(1969)

Reflux 1g cannabidiol, 60 mg p-toluenesulfonic acid (or 0.003 M trifluoroacetic acid) in 50 ml benzene for 1½ hours. Evaporate in vacuum to get about 0.7 g THC. Alternatively, add 1.8 g cannabidiol to 100 ml 0.005N HCl and reflux four hours. Proceed as above to get about 0.5 g THC [cf. JACS 94,6159(1972)].

*Nitrogen Analogs of* $\Delta^3$ *THC* CA 72,66922(1970); JACS 88, 3664(1966), TL 545(1972)

5.4 g olivetol or 0.03 M analog, 5.8 g 4-carbethoxy-N-benzyl-3-piperidone hydrochloride or 0.03 M analog [JACS 71,896 (1949) and 55,1239(1933) give an old and clumsy synthesis, and Heterocyclic Compounds, Klingenberg (Ed.), part 3, chaps. IX-XII (1962) gives information on related compounds] in 10 ml concentrated sulfuric acid. The concentrated sulfuric acid should be added dropwise, with cooling (cf. U.S. Patent 3,429, 889). Add 3 ml $POCl_3$ and stir at room temperature for 24 hours. Neutralize with $NaHCO_3$ to precipitate 2.3 g (I). Filter; wash precipitate with $NaHCO_3$ and recrystallize from acetonitrile. Dissolve 4.3 g (I) in 30 ml anisole and add 0.1 M methyl MgI in 50 ml anisole. Stir 12 hours and evaporate in vacuum or acidify with sulfuric acid, neutralize with $NaHCO_3$ and filter;

wash to get 2.4 g N-benzyl analog of THC. For other N-analogs of unknown activity see JOC *33*,2995(1968). Recover unreacted olivetol as usual.

The 5-aza analogs given in the JOC ref. seem to be active but they use the pyrone intermediate from certain routes of THC synthesis for a precursor. See U.S. Patent 3,493,579(03 Feb. 1970) for quinuclidine analogs and JOC *38*,440(1973) for a different approach to N-analogs. See JOC *39*,1546(1974) and HCA *56*,519(1973) for other N-analogs.

## $\Delta^{1\,(6)}$ THC U.S. Patent 3,576,887

This synthetic route allows one to proceed from the alkylresorcinol dimethyl ether without using a compound of the verbenol or cyclohexanone type.

Synthesis of olivetol aldehyde [Aust. J. Chem. *21*,2979 (1968)]. To a stirred solution of phenyllithium (1.6g bromobenzene and 0.16g Li) in 50 ml ether, add 0.01M olivetol dimethyl ether (or analog—see elsewhere here for preparation) in 5 ml ether and reflux 4 hours. Add 5 ml N-methylformanilide, reflux 1 hour and wash with 2X50 ml dilute sulfuric acid, 50 ml water, 25 ml saturated NaCl and dry, evaporate in vacuum the ether (can dissolve in benzene and filter through 100g of alumina) to get 60% yield of the dimethylolivetol aldehyde (I) (recrystallize from ether-pentane). Can recover unreacted starting material by refluxing the vacuum distillate 3 hours with excess 10% HCl, removing the organic layer and extracting the aqueous layer with ether: wash and dry, evaporate in vacuum the combined ether layers.

An alternative method for (I) [JACS *65*,361(1943)] In a 200 ml 3 neck round bottom flask with a stirrer, a reflux condenser, a dropping funnel and a nitrogen inlet tube, introduce a rapid stream of nitrogen and in the stream issuing from the central neck, cut 1.5g of lithium into ca. 70 pieces and drop into the flask containing about 25 ml dry ether. Place the fittings in position, slow the nitrogen stream and add ¼ of the solution of 9.2g n-butyl-chloride in 25 ml dry ether. Start the stirring and add the rest of the n-butyl-chloride at a rate giving a gentle reflux. Continue stirring and reflux 2 hours and add 15 ml olivetol dimethyl ether in 25 ml dry ether. Reflux 2 hours and add dropwise a solution of 15 ml N-methylformanilide in 25 ml dry ether with stirring at a rate sufficient to produce refluxing. Continue stirring 1 hour, treat with 3% sulfuric acid and then pour into excess of this acid. Remove upper layer and extract aqueous layer twice with ether. Wash combined ether layers with dilute aqueous $NaHCO_3$ and water and dry, evaporate in vacuum the ether (can distill 148-52/0.3) to get 78% (I).

JACS 65,361(1943). A mixture of 6.5g (I) (or analog), 20 ml pyridine, 1 ml piperidine and 9g malonic acid is warmed on a steam bath 1 hour. Add another 1g malonic acid and heat another ½ hour. Reflux ½ hour and pour into excess iced 10% HCl, stirring occasionally over 2 hours. Filter and dry to get 6g 2,6-dimethoxy-4-n-amylcinnamic acid (II) (recrystallize from ethanol).

10g (II), 40 ml 80% isoprene and 40 ml dry xylene or toluene is heated in an autoclave at 185° C for 15 hours. Cool, dilute with 160 ml petroleum ether and shake with 100 ml saturated aq. $Na_2CO_3$. Let stand and separate the middle layer. Wash the middle layer with a mixture of petroleum ether and dilute aq. $Na_2CO_3$ and again separate the middle layer and treat with 75 ml 10% HCl and 75 ml ether. Shake, separate the aqueous layer and wash the ether 3 times with water. Dry and evaporate in vacuum the ether and dissolve the residue in petroleum ether. The solid which ppts. after about 10 minutes is unchanged (II). Filter and let stand in refrigerator overnight and dry and evaporate in vacuum to ppt. about 7g of the 1-methyl-5(2,6-dimethoxy-4-n-amylphenyl)-1-cyclohexene-4-COOH (III) (recrystallize from petroleum ether).

1g (III) in 5 ml dry ether is added to 10 ml 3M MeMgI (from 0.21g Mg and 1.2g methyl iodide) in ether, heated to 130° C to evaporate the solvent and the oil kept at a bath temperature of 165° C for ½ hour. Cool in dry ice-acetone bath and cautiously add ammonium chloride-ice water mix to decompose the excess Grignard reagent. Acidify with dilute HCl and extract with ether. Wash with NaCl, dilute $K_2CO_3$, NaCl and dry, evaporate in vacuum to get the dimethyl derivative (IV). Reflux (IV) in 25 ml benzene with 100 mg p-toluenesulfonic acid for 1 hour with a Dean-Stark trap and dry, evaporate in vacuum (or wash with $NaHCO_3$, NaCl first) to get the THC or analog.

Hydrolysis of benzopyrones (for synthesis see elsewhere

here) will produce compounds of type (III) which will work in this synthesis. The hydrolysis proceeds as follows [JCS 926 (1927)]: Add 10g of the benzopyrone to 20g 30% NaOH, cool and shake 1 hour with 19 ml methylsulfate. Extract the oil with ether and dry, evaporate in vacuum to get the ester. Acidify the aqueous solution and filter, wash, dissolve ppt. in sodium carbonate and acidify, filter to get the free acid. Both the acid and the ester will work in this synthesis.

For a possible route to benzopyrones via condensation of isoprene and 3-CN-5-OH-7-alkyl-coumarin see JACS $82$,5198 (1960). See JMC $16$,1200(1973) for another ref. on the pyrone route to THC.

## $\Delta^3$ THC Analogs TET $23$,77(1967)

11.6 g 5-(1,2-dimethyl)-heptyl resorcinol or equimolar amount of olivetol or other analog, 9.2 g 2-carbethoxy-5-methyl cyclohexanone(4-carbethoxy-1-methyl-3-cyclohexanone), 5 g $POCl_3$, 70 ml dry benzene (protect from moisture with $CaCl_2$ tube). Boil 5 minutes (HCl evolution) and let stand at room temperature 20 hours. Pour into 10% $NaHCO_3$, separate the benzene layer and wash with 3X50 ml 10% $NaHCO_3$. Dry and evaporate in vacuum the benzene and recrystallize from 50 ml ethyl acetate to get 6.6 g of the pyrone (I). 4.5g(I), 150 ml benzene; add dropwise to a solution prepared from 7.8 g Mg, 18 ml methyl iodide, and 90 ml ether. Reflux 20 hours and add 45 ml saturated $NH_4Cl$. Separate the organic layer and extract the aqueous phase with benzene. Combine the organic layer and benzene and dry, evaporate in vacuum to get the THC analog.

## $\Delta^3$ THC Analogs from Resorcinol TET $23$,83(1967)

22g resorcinol, 36 g 4-carbethoxy-1-methyl-3-cyclohexanone, 20 g polyphosphoric acid; heat to 105° C and when the exothermic reaction which occurs subsides, heat at 140° C for one-half hour. Pour onto ice-water; filter; wash with water and recrystallize-ethanol to get 34 g of the pyrone (I). 6.4 g (I), 8 ml caproyl-Cl or analog (for preparation see above reference, page 84); heat on oil bath (can use mineral oil) at 120° C until the exothermic reaction subsides (HCl evolution). Cool and pour into ethanol. Filter to get 8 g precipitate (II). 3.2 g (II), 4.4 g dry $AlCl_3$; heat on oil bath at 170° C for one hour. Cool and add

HCl; filter and dissolve precipitate in 7 ml 2N NaOH. Filter and acidify with HCl to precipitate 1.4 g (III) (recrystallize-ethanol). Test this for activity. Use benzoyl-Cl or benzoic anhydride to esterify the OH group (this may not be necessary), methyl MgBr or methyl MgI to methylate the keto group, and sulfuric acid to dehydrate and hydrogenate as described elsewhere here to get the THC analog. Since the resulting THC analog has the side chain at the 6' position, it may not be active. This paper also gives a synthesis for THC analogs with the side chain in the 4' position, but again their activity in man is unknown. Verbenol, etc., should work in this synthesis, thus obviating the need for the methylation step.

## $\Delta^{1\,(6)}$ THC JACS 88,367(1966)

1M olivetol or analog, 1M citral in 10% $BF_3$ etherate in benzene about eight hours at 5-10° C. Extract unreacted olivetol with dilute NaOH and evaporate in vacuum the ether to get about 20% yield of the trans THC, and 20% of the cis THC which can be converted to the active trans isomer by reacting with $BBr_3$ in methylene chloride at -20° C for 1½ hours. [TL 4947(1969)]. Alternatively, the reaction can be carried out in 1% $BF_3$ etherate in methylene chloride to get 20% $\Delta^1$ THC.

## $\Delta^3$ THC Analogs JACS 63,1971(1941) cf. CA 82,170672-3 (1975)

7.6 g 5-n-heptyl resorcinol or equimolar amount analog, 6.6 g (0.037M) 4-carbethoxy-1-methyl-3-cyclohexanone or analog, 5.8 g $POCl_3$ in 60 ml benzene. Reflux 5 hours, cool and pour into $NaHCO_3$ to get about 6 g THC analog and 1 g more by concentrating the mother liquor, or proceed as described elsewhere here to recover unreacted resorcinol. 3-carbethoxy-1-methyl-2 or 4-cyclohexanone, 2-carbethoxy-cyclohexanone, etc. will probably also give active THC analogs.

## $\Delta^3$ THC Analogs JCS 952(1949)

1.75 g 2-Br-4-methyl-benzoic acid, 1.5 g olivetol or analog, 10 ml 1N Na OH and heat to boiling; add 0.5ml $CuSO_4$. Filter; wash with ethanol and recrystallize from ethanol to get (I). 10 g (I) in 150 ml benzene; add to methyl-MgI prepared from 47.5 g methyl iodide, 8 g Mg, 120 ml ether. Reflux fifteen hours, cool and pour on ice. Add saturated $NH_4Cl$ and separate the ether.

Wash two times with water and dry and evaporate in vacuum the ether to get the THC.

## PRECURSORS FOR THC SYNTHESIS

### p-Menthatriene (1,5,8) BER 89,2493(1956)

90 g d(+) carvone [ℓ (-) carvone or racemic carvone probably will work also] in 150 ml ether; add dropwise with stirring to 7.5 g lithium aluminum hydride in ether. Heat one hour on water bath; cool and carefully add water and then ice cold dilute sulfuric acid. Separate the ether and extract the aqueous layer with ether; dry and evaporate in vacuum the combined ether to get about 60 g product (can distill 65/14).

### (+) Cis and Trans p-Menthadien-(2,8)-ol-1

**Method 1:** LAC 674,93(1964) cf. BSC 3961(1971), JOC 38, 1684(1973)

136 g (+) limonene in 2 liters methanol; 2g bengal rose dye. Illuminate with a high voltage Hg lamp (e.g., HgH 5000) for fourteen hours or until about 1M of $O_2$ is taken up. Evaporate the methanol at 0-10° C to about 500 ml and then stir with ice cooling and add this solution dropwise to solution of 250 g $Na_2SO_3$ in 1.5 liters water and continue stirring for twelve hours. Heat two hours at 70° C and extract with ether and dry, evaporate in vacuum (can distill with addition of $Na_2CO_3$ at 40-70/0.2) to get about 100 g mixture containing about 40% product which can be purified by fractional distillation.

**Method 2:** HCA 48,1665(1965)

Convert (+) $\Delta^3$ carene to (+) trans-4-acetoxycarane (I) via (+) trans-4-OH-carane. Reflux 50 g (I) for 45 minutes (180° C oil bath under $N_2$ or Argon). Cool and can distill (57/10) to get about 25 g mixture of $\Delta^3$ and $\Delta^4$ carene (residue is unchanged starting material) containing about 60% $\Delta^4$ isomer.

Alternatively, to 150 ml ethylene diamine add portionwise with stirring at 110° C under Argon or $N_2$, 5.3 g Li metal; after one hour add dropwise 110 g (+) $\Delta^3$ carene. After one hour cool to 4° C and add water. Extract with ether, wash the ether five times with water and dry, evaporate in vacuum to get 100 g of a mix containing about 40% (+) $\Delta^4$ carene (can separate by fractional distillation).

$\Delta^4$ carene can also be obtained from $\Delta^3$ carene as follows: [JCS (C) 46(1966)]: Dissolve 1 g $\Delta^3$ carene in 50 ml propionic acid and heat at a suitable temperature (e.g., one-half hour at room temperature may do) in presence of ½ g Palladium-Carbon catalyst (5%) in ethanol and filter, evaporate in vacuum (can distill 63.5/19.5). See J. Soc. Cosmet. Chem. 22,249(1971) for a review of (+) $\Delta^3$ carene chemistry.

$\Delta^2$ *Carene oxide (2-epoxycarene)* LAC 687,22(1965), [cf. TL 2335(1966), and CA 68:22063(1968)]

To 136 g $\Delta^4$ carene in 330 ml methylene chloride and 120 g anhydrous sodium acetate, add dropwise with vigorous stirring in an ice bath, 167 g of 50% peracetic acid and continue stirring for ten hours. Heat to boiling for two hours, cool, wash with water, sodium carbonate, water, and dry, evaporate in vacuum the methylene chloride to get about 100 g p-menthadieneol. Apparently [CA 68,22063(1968)] substituting sodium carbonate for sodium acetate results in the production of $\Delta^2$ carene oxide (2-epoxycarene) in about 50% yield (can distill 63/7).

*4-Carbethoxy-1-methyl-cyclohexanone* LAC 630,78(1960)

Cool 20 g of sodium metal in 325 ml ethanol to -15° C in an ice-salt bath and add in small amounts over one hour a solution of 100 g 3-methyl-cyclohexanone and 150 g diethyloxalate (keep temperature below -10° C). Keep three hours in cold and then twelve hours at room temperature. Add solution of 1.3 L of water, 60 ml 2N sulfuric acid. Separate the yellow-brown oil and extract the water with ether or $CHCl_3$ until the yellow is removed. Combine the oil and the extract and distill the solvent and the unchanged starting material (100° C bath, 13 mm). Slowly heat the residue in a one-half liter flask with air cooling. $CO_2$ evolution starts at 160° C. Continue heating to 220° C and keep at this temperature for 1½ hours or until a test with 1% ethanol-$FeCl_3$ solution shows the end of the reaction by a violet color (unconverted material gives a brown color). Can distill two times on Vigreux column to give about 83 g of oily colorless product.

*(-) Verbenol* JCS 2232(1961)

Racemic alpha-pinene will yield racemic verbenol which will give one-half the yield of (-) verbenol.

27 g (-) alpha-pinene in 500 ml dry benzene; heat and keep temperature at 60-65° C throughout. Add with stirring over 20 minutes 84 g dry (dry over $P_2O_5$) lead tetra-acetate. Stir one-half hour; cool and filter and add filtrate to water. Filter and evaporate in vacuum the benzene layer (can distill 96-7/9) to get 21.2 g cis-2-acetoxy-pin-3-ene(I)). 5 g (I) in 25 ml glacial acetic acid; keep at 20° C for one-half hour and add water and extract with ether. Wash the extract with aqueous $Na_2CO_3$ and evaporate in vacuum the ether (can distill 97-8/9) to get 4.3 g trans verbenyl acetate (II). Hydrolyze (II) with NaOH to give the (-) cis and trans verbenol. For other methods of producing verbenol see CA 37,361(1943), CA 57,16772(1962) and BSC 2184(1964), JCS (B) 1259(1967). The last paper also gives a method for converting (-) beta-pinene to (-) alpha-pinene. See also CA 65,2312(66).

*5-Alkyl Resorcinols from Acyl Resorcinols* CA 72,66922(1970)

Compounds I-III may be able to give active THC analogs if used in place of olivetol for synthesis.

45 g 1-(3,5-dimethoxyphenyl)-1-hexanone(I) or analog (for preparation see the following methods) in 400 ml ether and 0.3 M methyl-MgI in 150 ml ether react to give 49 g 2-(3,5-dimethoxyphenyl)-2-heptanol(II). Heat 49g (II) with 1 ml 20% sulfuric acid to 105-125° C/30 mm for 1½ hours to get 34 g of the 2-heptene compound (III). 33g (III) in 100 ml ethanol, 6g Raney-Ni, 1500 PSI hydrogen, 150° C to get 26 g of the 2-heptane (IV). 26 g (IV), 118 ml 57% hydrogen iodide; add 156 ml acetic anhydride and heat at 155° C for two hours to get 22 g of the resorcinol.

*5-Alkyl Resorcinols* BER 69,1644(1936)

25 g ethyl-3,4,5-trimethoxybenzoyl acetate and 2.1 g Na in 100 ml ethanol; warm to react. Add 2 g n-propyl iodide (or n-amyl iodide, etc.) and heat twelve hours on steam bath; neutralize and distill off the ethanol. Extract with ether and dry, evaporate in vacuum to get about 32 g of the alkyl acetate (I). Heat 22 g (I) in 5% KOH in ethanol for one hour at 50° C to get 14 g 3,4,5-trimethoxyvalerophenone (II), which crystallizes on standing. 11 g (II), 600 ml ethanol, 60 g Na; warm and after Na is dissolved, add 2 L water. Acidify with HCl, distill off the ethanol and extract with ether. Dry, evaporate in vacuum the ether to

get 7.8 g olivetol dimethyl ether (or analog) (III). 7.2 g (III), 70 ml hydrogen iodide; boil two hours and distill (164/760) to get olivetol.

## Olivetol HCA 52,1132(1969)

Reduce 3,5-dimethoxybenzoic acid with lithium aluminum hydride to 3,5-dimethoxybenzyl alcohol (I). To 10.5 g(I) in 100 ml methylene chloride at 0° C add 15 g $PBr_3$; warm to room temperature and stir for one hour. Add a little ice water and then more methylene chloride. Separate and then dry, evaporate in vacuum the methylene chloride. Add petroleum ether to precipitate about 11.5 g of the benzyl bromide (II). To 9.25 g (II), 15 g CuI, 800 ml ether at 0° C, add butyl (or other alkyl)-Li (16% in hexane), and stir for four hours at 0° C. Add saturated $NH_4Cl$ and extract with ether. Dry and evaporate in vacuum the ether (can distill 100/0.001) to get about 4.5 g olivetol dimethyl ether (III) or analog. Distill water from a mixture of 90 ml pyridine, 100 ml concentrated HCl until temperature is 210° C. Cool to 140° C and add 4.4 g (III); reflux two hours under $N_2$. Cool and pour into water. Extract with ether and wash with $NaHCO_3$. Make pH 7 and dry, evaporate in vacuum to get 3.8 g olivetol which can be chromatographed on 200 g silica gel (elute with $CHCl_3$) or distill (130/0.001) to purify.

## 5-Alkyl Resorcinols TET 23,77(1967)

Since the method as given originally leads to 4-alkyl resorcinols which do not produce an active THC, it is here modified to give the 5-alkyl isomers. The method is illustrated for 1.2-dimethylheptyl resorcinol which gives a much more active THC than olivetol.

Convert 3,5-dihydroxyacetophenone (5-acetyl resorcinol) to 3,5-dimethoxyacetophenone(I) in the usual way with dimethylsulfate.

To 24 g Mg, 1 crystal $I_2$, 100 ml ether, add dropwise under $N_2$, 180 g 2-Br-heptane in 100 ml ether over one hour and then reflux two hours. Add over 1½ hours a solution of 90g (I) in 200 ml tetrahydrofuran and reflux 10 hours. Cool and add 180 ml saturated $NH_4Cl$; decant the solvents and extract the residue with tetrahydrofuran. Combine the solvents and the tetrahydrofuran and dry, evaporate in vacuum. Add a few drops 20% sul-

furic acid to the residual oil and evaporate in vacuum the water
(oil bath temperature 120-130° C/10 mm). Distill the oil at oil
bath temperature 285° C/0.2. Fraction boiling 128-140/0.2
yields about 60 g 2-(3,5-dimethoxyphenyl)-3-methyl-2-octene
(II). If saponified and used to synthesize a THC, this might give
an active product, thus disposing of the necessity of the next
step. Hydrogenate 50 g (II) in 100 ml ethanol, 2-3 atmospheres
$H_2$, 0.6 g 10% Palladium-Carbon catalyst for two hours, or until
no more $H_2$ uptake (or use the $NaBH_4$-Ni method described at
the start). Filter and dry, evaporate in vacuum, and distill the
residual oil (110-17/0.1) to get 42 g of the octane (III). 40 g
(III), 100 ml 48% HBr, 320 ml glacial acetic acid and reflux
four hours. Pour on ice and take pH to 4.5 with 10 N NaOH
and extract with ether. Extract the ether with 3X150 ml 2N
NaOH; acidify the combined NaOH extracts with glacial acetic
acid and extract with ether. Dry and evaporate in vacuum, and
distill the oil (159/0.1) to get 20 g 5-1, 2-dimethylheptyl resorcinol.

*5-Alkyl Resorcinols* JACS *61,*232(1939)

Convert benzoic acid to 3,5-dihydroxybenzoic acid (alpha-resor-
cylic acid) (I). 50 g (I), 134 g dimethylsulfate, 60 g NaOH,
300 ml water; add 35 g NaOH and reflux to obtain about 50 g
3,5-dimethoxybenzoic acid (II) which is converted to dimeth-
oxybenzoyl chloride (III) with $PCl_5$. Extract the (III) with
ether and filter. Saturate the ether with $NH_3$ at 0° C and filter.
Wash with ether and water and recrystallize from hot water to
get 3,5-dimethoxybenzamide (IV). To a solution of 1 M of n-
hexyl bromide (or 1,2-dimethylheptyl bromide, etc.) add 24.3 g
Mg in 200 ml ether to prepare the Grignard reagent. Then
rapidly add 46 g (IV); add 300 ml ether and reflux and stir two
days, excluding moisture and air. Add a mixture of ice and
water and 80 ml concentrated sulfuric acid. Separate and dry,
evaporate in vacuum the ether layer to get about 50 g of the
dimethoxyyalkyl benzyl ketone (V). Recrystallize from dilute
ethanol. Add 0.2 M (V), 20.8 g 100% hydrazine hydrate, 75 ml
ethanol; reflux six hours. Evaporate in vacuum and heat the residual oil with 82 g powdered KOH in oil bath about 225° C
until $N_2$ evolution ceases. Can distill or recrystallize from 95%
ethanol to get the dimethoxyalkyl benzene (VI). 0.025 M (VI),

40 ml glacial acetic acid, 15 ml 48% HBr; reflux four hours and pour into ice water; decolorize with a little Na bisulfite, neutralize with NaHCO$_3$ and extract with ether. Wash the extract with 10% NaOH and separate and acidify the basic solution. Extract with ether and dry, evaporate in vacuum the extract to get the 5-alkyl resorcinol. Distill or recrystallize from water to purify. Dry, evaporate in vacuum the first ether extract to recover starting material.

*Olivetol* LAC *630,*77(1960), JCS 311(1945), cf. JACS *89,*6734 (1967)

Dissolve 100 g malonic acid in 360 g dry pyridine and heat 48-52° C for forty hours with 100 g n-hexaldehyde (n-capronaldehyde) or homolog. Cool in ice bath and with good stirring add dropwise 150 ml ice cold concentrated sulfuric acid (keep temperature below 5° C). After addition add water to dissolve the precipitate and extract with ether two times. Dry, evaporate in vacuum the ether and distill (70/0.7 or 102/5) to get about 98 g 2-octenoic acid (I). 95 g (I) in 300 ml ether; cool to -5° C and slowly add a solution of an excess of diazomethane in ether dried over KOH and let react for about one hour. Let stand twelve hours, evaporate in vacuum and distill (91/17) to get about 94 g clear methyl-2-octenoate (II).

To 16.3 g Na in 210 ml ethanol add 93 g ethyl-acetoacetate (ethyl-3-oxo-butanoate), heat to boil and add dropwise 92 g (II) over 20 minutes. Stir and reflux five hours and cool to precipitate. Filter, wash with ethanol and dissolve precipitate in 800 ml water. Cool to 0° C and slowly add 80 ml ice cold concentrated HCl to precipitate. Filter, wash with water and ligroin to get about 108 g 6-carbethoxy-4,5-dihydro-olivetol (III) (recrystallize from petroleum ether). To 104 g (III) in 260 ml glacial acetic acid at room temperature with good stirring, add dropwise over one hour 69 ml Bromine. Heat four to five hours at 60° C, cool and add 300 ml water and let stand twelve hours. Oil separates which will precipitate on agitation and rubbing. Filter, wash with water until colorless (recrystallize from ligroin, recrystallize from glacial acetic acid and precipitate with water) to get about 86 g 6-carbethoxy-2,4-dibromo-olivetol (IV). 0.035 g Palladium-Carbon catalyst in 25 ml hydrogenation bottle. Saturate with H$_2$ (pressure - 2.8 Kg/cm$^2$) and add 0.33g

(IV) in 5 ml glacial acetic acid, which takes up 39.5 cm³ $H_2$ at atmospheric pressure over 1½ hours at 60-70° C. Filter and acidify at 0° C with ice cold 6N HCl. Extract with ether and dry, evaporate in vacuum. Recrystallize the oil from ligroin and then from glacial acetic acid by adding water to get about 0.2 g 6-carbethoxyolivetol (V). (IV) can also be hydrogenated at room temperature and atmospheric pressure over ½g Palladium-Carbon catalyst by dissolving 70 g in 500 ml 1N NaOH. Heat 35 g (V) with 45 g NaOH in 170 ml water for two hours or until no more $CO_2$ is evolved. Cool, acidify with 6N HCl and boil 3 minutes. Extract the oil with ether and dry, evaporate in vacuum the ether (can distill on Vigreux column 123/0.01, oil bath 160° C) and let oil stand in refrigerator until crystalline to get about 21 g olivetol. See CA 70,77495t(1969) for another variant of this procedure.

*1',1'-Dimethylolivetol* HCA 52,1127(1969)

Prepare 3,5 dimethoxy benzyl alcohol by reducing the acid with lithium aluminum hydride as described elsewhere here, by hydrogenating the aldehyde (2-3 atmospheres $H_2$, room temperature, $PtO_2$ in ethanol—or by the $NaBH_4$ method), in five steps as described in JACS 70,666(1948), or prepare (II) directly by the diborane procedure.

Add with stirring 22.5 g $SOCl_2$ in 100 ml ether in 20 ml portions to a solution of 15 g 3,5-dimethoxybenzyl alcohol, 1 ml pyridine and 200 ml ether. Let stand and wash with 2X100 ml cold water; separate and dry, evaporate in vacuum the ether to get 16 g 3,5-dimethoxybenzyl chloride (I). Recrystallize from petroleum ether. 16 g (I), 300 ml ethanol, 30 g NaCN, 75 ml water; reflux three hours and pour onto 400 g ice. After ice melts, filter and recrystallize precipitate from petroleum ether to get about 14 g 3,5-dimethoxybenzyl CN (II). 5g 50% NaH in mineral oil; wash three times with pentane or hexane; fill flask with $N_2$ or argon and add dimethoxyethane or dimethylformamide (freshly distilled from K if possible). Stir and add 9 ml methyl iodide. Carefully add 8 g (II) and stir twelve hours. Add ice water and neutralize with $NaHCO_3$ to pH 7-8. Extract with ether and dry, evaporate in vacuum the ether (can distill 170/0.1) to get about 9 g alpha, alpha-dimethyl-3,5-dimethoxyphenylacetonitrile (III). Add 1.5 g (III) to a solution of 0.45 g Mg,

2.5 g n-propyl Br (freshly distilled if possible) in 30 ml ether. Reflux sixty-five hours. Add 2N sulfuric acid and heat two hours on water bath. Cool and extract with ether and dry, evaporate in vacuum (can distill 135/0.001) to get about 1.75 g 2-methyl-2-(3,5-dimethoxyphenyl) hexanone-3 (IV). Dissolve 4 g (IV) in 50 g ethane dithiol and saturate at 0° C with HCl gas (take care to exclude water). Stir the solution in a sealed container forty-eight hours at room temperature and then basify with $NaHCO_3$. Extract with ether and dry, evaporate in vacuum (or dry and evaporate in vacuum two hours at 70/12 and distill at 130/0.001) to get about 5 g of the thioketal (V). Reflux 5.3 g (V), 100 g Raney-Ni, 2 L ethanol (or use $NaBH_4$ procedure) for thirty hours. Cool and filter (Celite), evaporate in vacuum and distill residue (115/0.001) to get 3.7 g of the hexane which is saponified as described for the dimethyl ether of olivetol above to give about 2.5 g of the title compound (can distill 150/0.001).

*Olivetol* ACS 24,716(1970)

Prepare 3,5-dimethoxybenzoic acid as described elsewhere here, and to a solution of 18.2 g in 250 ml dry tetrahydrofuran under $N_2$, add 1 g 85% LiH, stir for fourteen hours and then reflux for one-half hour. Add a solution of about 1.3 M butyllithium in ether [Org. Rxns. 6,352(1957)] with stirring and ice cooling until the reaction mixture gives a positive Gilman test [JACS 47, 2002(1925)]. Then add 500 ml ice water, extract with ether and dry, evaporate in vacuum the organic phase to get a yellow oil which is dissolved in an equal amount of absolute ethanol; left in refrigerator twelve hours to precipitate. Filter and evaporate in vacuum the ethanol to one-half volume to give more precipitate for a total of 18 g 1-(3,5-dimethoxyphenyl)-1 pentanone (I). 5.64 g(I) in 200 ml methanol; 0.66 g 20% Pd(OH)$_2$ on carbon [TL 1663(1967)] and hydrogenate at room temperature and atmospheric pressure over two to three hours (or use other reducing method as described here). Filter and evaporate in vacuum to get olivetol dimethyl ether (II). 4.88 g (II), 40 ml HI (density 1.7, decolorized with red phosphorous) and stir three hours at 115-125° C under $N_2$. Dry, evaporate in vacuum or pour into 100 ml ice water and extract with methylene chloride; wash methylene chloride with water and dry, evaporate in vacuum (can distill 160-170/3-4) to get 3.5 g olivetol.

*5-Alkyl Resorcinols* JOC *33*,687(1968), JACS *71*,1624,1628 (1949)

Illustrated for 1,2-dimethylheptyl compound.

110 g powdered 3,5-dimethoxybenzamide (preparation given elsewhere here), five times excess of methylMgI and reflux sixteen hours. Add 1.2 L concentrated HCl and 1200 g ice and let stand sixteen hours with occasional shaking. Extract with ether, dry, evaporate in vacuum and distill (115-128/0.3). Let stand in refrigerator to precipitate. Wash precipitate with petroleum ether and recrystallize from petroleum ether to get about 60 g 3,5-dimethoxyacetophenone (I). 83 g (I) in 50 ml methanol. Add dropwise with stirring to solution of 18 g $NaBH_4$ in 300 ml methanol and 1 g NaOH. Reflux 30 minutes and concentrate by distilling. Add about 100 ml water during distillation. Evaporate the methanol, cool and extract with ether. Dry, filter, concentrate, and distill (124/0.65) to get about 80 g 3,5-dimethoxyphenyl ethanol (II). 18 ml $PBr_3$ in 70 ml ether; add dropwise with stirring over one hour to 28.5 g (II) in 70 ml ether cooled in an ice bath. Warm to room temperature; reflux two hours on steam bath; cool and pour into 200 g ice. Shake and extract with ether 3 times; wash ether with 10% $NaHCO_3$ and water and dry, filter. Concentrate on steam bath and then add with stirring under anhydrous conditions to 42 g diethyl-n-amylmalonate in 300 ml ethanol in which has been dissolved 4.6 g Na metal. Stir 1½ hours at room temperature and then heat to distill off the ether and complete the reaction. When the distillation head temperature reaches 78°C add water and continue distilling until temperature reaches 99° C. Cool and extract with 3X250 ml ether and evaporate in vacuum the ether. Dissolve residue in 180 ml ethylene glycol and 35 g NaOH by stirring six hours at 160° C. Cool and add 1500 ml water and wash with ether. Acidify the aqueous phase and extract with 4X200 ml ether. Evaporate in vacuum the ether or evaporate on steam bath and dissolve the residue in 150 ml xylene. Evaporate residual ether and water until head temperature reaches 140° C and reflux six hours. Evaporate in vacuum to get about 30 g oily alpha-amyl-beta-methyl-hydrocinnamic acid (III). 14.5 g (III), 5 g lithium aluminum hydride, 250 ml ether; reflux 6 hours. Cool and carefully add methanol, water and dilute HCl. Separate the aqueous layer, saturate with NaCl and extract with ether. Wash ether

with NaHCO$_3$ (acidify NaHCO$_3$ extract to precipitate starting
material) and dry, evaporate in vacuum the ether to get about
12 g 2-amyl-3(3,5-dimethoxyphenyl)-butanol (IV). 11.7 g (IV)
and 8.5 g p-toluenesulfonyl Cl each dissolved in 20 ml pyridine.
Cool in ice bath and combine. Place in freezer about sixteen
hours, pour over ice and extract with ether. Wash ether with
cool, dilute HCl until HCl extract is acidic. The combined HCl
extracts are then acidified and extracted with ether. Wash the
ether with NaHCO$_3$, dry and then add dropwise with stirring to
3 g lithium aluminum hydride in 75 ml ether. Reflux 4½ hours
and work up as for (IV). (Can chromatograph the undistilled
product on activated alumina and elute with 600 ml petroleum
ether, then 200 ml methanol; concentrate and distill (94/0.001)
the petroleum ether to get product; concentrate the methanol
to give starting material). Yield is about 8 g 2-(3,5-dimethoxy-
phenyl)-3-methyl-octane (V). Convert (V) to the title compound
by refluxing in 48% HBr in glacial acetic acid as described elsewhere here.

An alternative route from (II) to (V) involves adding (II) and
diethylmethylmalonate to prepare dimethyl-3,5-dimethoxyhy-
drocinnamic acid as described for the preparation of (III). Then
dehydrate and hydrolyze to dimethyl-3,5-dimethoxycinnamic
acid which is hydrogenated to the alcohol and converted in several steps to (V).

*5-Alkylresorcinols* Aust. J. Chem. *21*,2979(1968)

Reflux 6.9 g triphenylphosphine and 6.6g lauryl bromide (or
equimolar amount of homolog) in 40 ml xylene for 60 hours.
Remove solvent and wash residue with 5X20 ml ether (by de-
canting) to get 11g lauryl triphenylphosphonium bromide(I).
To a stirred suspension of 5.6g(0.011M)(I) in 50 ml ether add
0.01M butyllithium solution [see Organic Reactions *8*,258
(1954) for preparation].Stir ½ hour at room temperature and
slowly add 1.66g 3,5-dimethoxybenzaldehyde (preparation
given elsewhere here) in 10 ml ether over ½ hour. After 15
hours, filter, wash filtrate with water and dry, evaporate in vacuum. Dilute residue with pentane, filter and remove solvent. Dissolve the residual oil in 25 ml ethyl acetate and hydrogenate
over 0.1g Adams catalyst at one atmosphere and room temperature for 2 hours. Filter and evaporate in vacuum to get the 5-

alkylresorcinol dimethyl ether which can be recrystallized from pentane and demethylated as described elsewhere here.

*5-Alkylresorcinols* Aust. J. Chem. *21*,2979(1968)

Add 2.17g 3,5-dimethoxybenzoyl chloride [see BER *41*,1329 (1908) or elsewhere here for preparation] in 2.5 ml ether over 10 minutes to a stirred solution of 0.42g diazomethane and 1.01 g triethylamine in ether at -5° C. Keep 10 hours at 0° C, filter, wash precipitate with 20 ml ether and evaporate in vacuum the combined filtrates to get 1.9g diazo-3,5-dimethoxyace-tophenone(I). Recrystallize from benzene-cyclohexane. To 1.5g(I) in 15 ml ethanol add 1.23g pyridinium perchlorate in 2 ml pyridine. Reflux 2 hours, cool and add 5 ml water. Filter to get 1.5g 3,5-dimethoxyphenylacyl pyridinium perchlorate (II). Recrystallize from ethanol. To a stirred suspension of 0.13 g Na hydride in 10 ml dry, acid free dimethylacetamide at 10° C under nitrogen, add 1.79g (II) in 10 ml dimethylacetamide and shake for 15 minutes. Add 0.0075M propyl iodide or homolog and keep 12 hours at room temperature. Heat 2 hours at 90° C and cool to room temperature. Add 3g zinc dust and 5 ml gla-cial acetic acid; stir at room temperature four hours and filter. Add 20 ml water to filtrate and extract with 50 ml ether. Wash the ether layer with 2X50 ml 10% $K_2CO_3$, 50 ml water and 20 ml saturated NaCl. Dry and evaporate in vacuum to get oily 3, 5-dimethoxyphenylbutyl ketone (can chromatograph on 50g alumina and elute with 3:1 petroleum ether:ether). Recrystal-lize from methanol. Hydrogenolysis [see Aust. J. Chem. *18*, 2015(1965) or elsewhere here] gives the olivetol dimethyl ether.

*5-Alkylresorcinols* Aust. J. Chem. *24*,2655(1971)

The method is illustrated for olivetol preparation, but substi-tuted thiophens can be used to get olivetol homologs.

To a stirred solution of 45g 3,5-dimethoxybenzoyl chloride and 17.4g thiophen in 300 ml benzene at 0° C, add dropwise 10.5g freshly distilled stannic chloride. Stir one hour at room temperature and add 200 ml 3% aqueous HCl. Separate the ben-zene layer and wash the aqueous layer with benzene. Dry and evaporate in vacuum the combined benzene layers and distill the red residue (250° C bath/4.5) to get 45g 2-(3,5-dimethoxy-

benzoyl) thiophen(I). Recrystallize from petroleum ether. Add
a solution of 21g AlCl$_3$ in 160 ml ether to a stirred suspension
of 6.1g lithium aluminum hydride in 140 ml ether. After 5 minutes add a solution of 39g (I) in 300 ml ether at a rate giving a
gentle reflux. Reflux and stir 1 hour; cool in an ice bath and
treat dropwise with 50 ml water, then 50 ml 6N aqueous sulfuric acid. Separate the layers, extract the aqueous layer with 3X
100 ml ether and dry, evaporate in vacuum the combined ether
layers. Can distill the residue (230° C bath/5mm) to get 27g
oily 2-(3,5-dimethoxybenzyl) thiophen(II). Recrystallize from
petroleum ether. Reflux a solution of 5g (II) in 700 ml ethanol
with W-7 Raney Nickel prepared from Ni-Al alloy [see Org.
Synthesis Coll. Vol. *III*,176(1955)] for 6 hours. Filter, evaporate in vacuum and can distill (140/0.01) to get about 2.2g oily
olivetol dimethyl ether which can be reduced to olivetol as described elsewhere here. The use of the novel reduction methods
described at the beginning of this section would render this
method much simpler.

*5-Alkylresorcinols* German Patent 2,002,815 (30 July 1970)

In a 2 liter, 3 necked flask with a stirrer, dropping funnel, thermometer, reflux head, nitrogen stream and mercury manometer
(if available) stir 230 ml dry methanol and 32.4g sodium methoxide under nitrogen until dissolved. Add 110g diethylmalonate
and stir 10 minutes. Add portionwise 75g 90% pure 3-nonene-
2-one (for olivetol-preparation below) keeping the temperature
below the boiling point (50-60° C). Stir and reflux 3 hours,
then cool to room temperature, neutralize with about 50 ml
concentrated HCl and let stand overnight. Evaporate in a vacuum and dissolve the residue in 200 ml 1N HCl and 800 ml ethylacetate. Separate and wash the ethylacetate with 2X300 ml
water and extract with saturated NaHCO$_3$ until a small portion
gives no turbidity upon acidification (about 5X200 ml). Carefully acidify the combined NaHCO$_3$ extracts and then extract
with 3X300 ml ether. Dry and evaporate in vacuum the ether
(can dry under vacuum several days) to get 6-n-pentyl-2-OH-4-
oxo-cyclohex-2-ene-1-methyl-carboxylate (I). 4.8g (I) and 100
ml glacial acetic acid are stirred vigorously at 75° C until dissolved. Cool and keep temperature between 5 and 10° C while
adding a solution of 3.9g bromine in 10 ml glacial acetic acid

dropwise over 1 hour. Stir 1 hour at room temperature then 3 hours on a steam bath. Evaporate in vacuum and dissolve the residual oil in 200 ml ether. Wash with 2X25 ml 10% sodium dithionite, 2X25 ml saturated $NaHCO_3$ and water and dry, evaporate in vacuum to get olivetol (or analog) (can distill at 125-130/0.05).

Alternatively, to 4.8g (I) add 5.6g iodine in 200 ml glacial acetic acid. Stir and reflux 10 hours, evaporate in vacuum, dissolve residue in 250 ml ether and proceed as above to get olivetol.

A third alternative is to stir 12.2g (I) in 100 ml glacial acetic acid at 25° C with vigorous stirring until well suspended. Cool and keep temperature at 5-10° C while adding dropwise 22.4g cupric bromide dissolved in 25 ml glacial acetic acid over 1 hour. Stir 1 hour at room temperature then 3 hours on a steam bath and evaporate in vacuum. Dissolve the residue in 200 ml water and 300 ml ether. Wash the ether layer with 2X50 ml 10% sodium dithionite, 2X35 ml saturated $NaHCO_3$ and 75 ml water and dry, evaporate in vacuum to get olivetol (or analog).

For the 1,2-dimethylheptyl homolog proceed as follows. Combine 15g 5,6-dimethylundec-3-ene-2-one with 19g diethylmalonate as described above to get (I). Brominate 20.2g (I) with 12g bromine over 2 hours as described and stir 1 hour at room temperature. Add 500 ml water and let stand overnight at 5-10° C. Filter, wash precipitate with about 4X75 ml cold water and dry in vacuum at 50° C to get 26g 3-bromo-2-OH-4-oxo-6 (1,2-dimethylheptyl)-cyclohex-2-ene-1-methylcarboxylate (II). In a 3 liter 3 necked flask with a stirrer, thermometer, reflux head and Dean-Stark trap, add 350g (II) and 522g pyridine hydrochloride and heat on oil bath at 90° C 4 hours. Heat with the heating mantle (removing volatiles with the Dean-Stark trap) until the internal temperature reaches 190-200° C and hold at this temperature 2 hours. Cool to room temperature and shake with 3 liters ether and 660 ml 1.2N HCl. Separate and wash the ether layer with 300 ml 1.2N HCl and then 2X300 ml water. Extract the ether solution with 4X350 ml 10% NaOH and then extract the combined NaOH extracts with 2X300 ml ether. Acidify the alkaline solution with about 700 ml concentrated HCl and extract with 3X800 ml ether. Wash the combined ether extracts with 3X300 ml 10% sodium dith-

ionite, 2X300 ml saturated NaHCO₃ and 300 ml water and dry,
evaporate in vacuum the ether to get the 5-(1,2-dimethyl-heptyl)
resorcinol.

To prepare the 3-nonene-2-one condense excess acetone
with n-hexaldehyde (or 2,3-dimethyloctanal for 5,6-dimethyl-
undec-3-ene-2-one) in the presence of NaOH in an inert medium if desired (benzene, toluene, xylene, etc.), at 10-70° C to
get (I). Dehydrate (I) with sodium sulfate or cupric sulfate in an
inert medium at reflux temperature or simply reflux in benzene,
xylene or toluene.

## 5-Alkylresorcinols JOC 37,2901(1972)

For 5-alkylresorcinols see Chem. and Ind. 685(1973) also.

This is an improved version of a previously given synthesis
(LAC 630,71(1960)). The ethanol used is distilled from Ca
ethoxide; dimethoxyethane from potassium. Cupric bromide is
produced from cupric oxide and 5% excess of HBr, plus sufficient bromine to remove the milkiness on addition of a drop of
the mixture to water; concentrate and dry, evaporate in vacuum
over KOH flakes.

650g (5.3M) ethyl chloroacetate and 880g (5.3M) triethyl
phosphite are mixed and placed in a 3 liter flask fitted with a
thermometer and condenser under nitrogen. Heat and stir and
slowly bring to 125° C. Discontinue heating as ethyl chloride
evolution proceeds over ½ hour. Heat to 160° C over a 75 minute period and keep at 160° C 8 hours. Cool, distill (e.g.,
through 12″ Vigreux column) (74-7/0.03) to get 96% yield of
triethylphosphonoacetate (I). In a 3 liter flask fitted with a stirrer, dropping funnel and condenser, place 45.3g NaH (1M in
mineral oil) and 1 liter of dry ether. Flush with nitrogen and
keep at positive nitrogen pressure. Stir in ice bath while 224 g
(1M) (I) is added dropwise over 75 min. Stir and reflux 1 hour
(H₂ evolution stops). Cool in ice-salt bath and add 1M of aldehyde (e.g., hexaldehyde for olivetol) over 1 hour. Continue to
cool and stir an additional 10 minutes and then slowly bring to
reflux and reflux for 10 minutes (ppt. prevents stirring). Decant
the ether and dissolve the oil layer in 500 ml warm water and
separate the upper organic layer. Extract the aqueous layer with
200 ml ether and extract the combined organic solutions with
200 ml saturated NaHCO₃. Dry and evaporate in vacuum (can

distill) to get the ethyl-β-alkylacrylates in about 90% yield (II).

In a flask with nitrogen and fittings as in preceding step, add 156 g ethyl acetoacetate to Na ethoxide from 25.3g Na and 500 ml dry ethanol, and stir and reflux ½ hour. Add 1M of (II) dropwise over 90 minutes and reflux 20 hours. Cool in ice, filter, wash ppt with 500 ml ice cold absolute ethanol and several times with portions of ether and dry, evaporate in vacuum to get the dione Na salt (III) in about 80% yield (for olivetol precursor). In a 250 ml flask place 0.1M (III), 100 ml 1,2-dimethoxyethane and flush with nitrogen and stir at room temperature while 45g of cupric bromide is added portionwise over 5 minutes, under a nitrogen stream. Stir ½ hour and then reflux and stir 1 hour. Cool and evaporate (keep temperature below 50° C) but do not remove more than about 65 ml dimethoxyethane. Dilute the remaining solution with 200 ml benzene and filter. Wash the ppt. with 50 ml benzene and evaporate the combined benzene filtrates (keep temperature below 50° C). Dissolve the bromodione in 100 ml dimethylformamide and put in 500 ml flask under nitrogen. Stir and heat slowly until reflux and then heat to 150° C and reflux 4 hours. Cool, pour into 500 ml water, extract with 3X100 ml dichloromethane and dry, evaporate in vacuum to get the ethyl-6-alkyl-2,4-dihydroxybenzoate (IV). Add a solution of 24g NaOH in 200 ml water to (IV) and stir and reflux under nitrogen in hood for 3 hours. Cool in ice bath, acidify carefully with a cold solution of 20 ml concentrated sulfuric acid in 80 ml water while stirring under nitrogen in ice bath. Reflux under nitrogen 5 minutes, cool, extract 3 times with ether and dry, evaporate in vacuum the combined extracts to get about 80% yield of olivetol (or analog). The last step may not be necessary since (IV) may yield an active THC.

*Dimethylheptylresorcinol* CA 65,20062(1966)

This method is specifically designed to produce good yields of dimethylheptylresorcinol, which provides, after synthesis by any of the various routes, one of the most active THC analogs yet discovered. Note that the synthesis may not have to be carried all the way to the alkylresorcinol since the intermediate ketones etc. may give an active THC analog.

Mix 294g (1.6M) 1,3,5-trichlorobenzene, 184g (3.4M) Na methoxide and 450g (3.3M) diglyme and reflux at 162° C for

42 hours. Cool to room temperature, filter and distill the solvent to get 70% yield of 1-Cl-3,5-dimethoxybenzene (I). 43.2g (I) in 540 ml tetrahydrofuran is added dropwise to 7.3g Mg, a small crystal of iodine and a few drops of ethyl bromide (under nitrogen if possible) over ½ hour while the mixture is heated to 75° C. Reflux 2 hours and cool to room temperature to obtain the Grignard solution.

To anhydrous liquid ammonia in a cooled flask, add $Fe(NO_3)_3 \cdot 9H_2O$ and then small pieces of sodium and bubble air through the solution until reaction is observed. Add more sodium portionwise until 11.5g is in solution. To the solution at its reflux temperature, add 27.6g (0.5M) proprionitrile (or isobutyronitrile etc. for analogs) and add the resulting solution dropwise to 53.3g 1-Cl-pentane (or 0.5M analog such as 2-Br-hexane etc.) and let the ammonia evaporate. Add ether, then water to the residue and separate the aqueous layer and extract with ether. Dry and evaporate in vacuum the combined ether solutions to give 64% yield of 2-methylheptanonitrile (II) (or analog).

Add 34.0g (0.27M) (II) in tetrahydrofuran to the Grignard solution of (I) over ½ hour, heat 6 hours at 60° C and hydrolyze with 1600 ml 50% sulfuric acid, keeping the temperature below 40° C. Evaporate in vacuum the solvent and add another 400 ml 50% sulfuric acid. Heat 1 hour at 95-100° C, cool, add ether, separate the aqueous layer and extract with ether. Dry and evaporate in vacuum the combined ether layers to get 71% yield 2-(3,5-dimethoxybenzoyl) heptane (III) (can distill 133-8/0.2), which can be demethylated as described for the preparation of (VII) below and possibly used to synthesize an active THC analog (as can IV, V, or VI).

21.8g (0.082M) (III) is added dropwise (keeping the temperature at 15-20° C) to 3 molar methyl-MgBr in ether and refluxed 1 hour. Pour into a sulfuric acid-ice mix, add more sulfuric acid and stir. Separate and extract the aqueous layer with ether. Wash, dry, filter and evaporate in vacuum the combined ether layers to get 2-(3,5-dimethoxyphenyl)-3-methyl-octanol (IV), which is dehydrated by mixing with anhydrous oxalic acid and heating to 130-40° C. Extract the dehydrated reaction products with benzene to get the octenes (V). Add 25g (V), 2.5g

65% Ni on kieselguhr in dry hexane to hydrogenator and hydrogenate at 1750 psi and gradually increase the temperature to 125° C. After 3 hours, increase the pressure to 1850 psi and hold there 2½ hours. Filter and evaporate in vacuum to get 2-(3,5-dimethoxyphenyl)-3-methyl-octane (VI).

Add 20g (0.08M) (VI) to 38% HBr in glacial acetic acid and stir and reflux for 6 hours. Pour onto ice and water, neutralize with solid sodium carbonate and extract with ether. Extract the ether with 10% aqueous NaOH, acidify the aqueous solution with HCl, extract with ether and dry, evaporate in vacuum (can distill) to get 2-(3,5-dihydroxyphenyl)-3-methyloctane (VII) (5-(1,2-dimethylheptyl)-resorcinol).

As an alternative process for getting from (III) to (VI), combine 64.2g (0.18M) methyltriphenylphosphonium bromide in dry benzene with 11.6g (0.18M) (in 14% solution) butyllithium in benzene. Heat to 60° C and cool. 49.0g (0.176M) (III) in 40 ml dry benzene is added (keep temperature below 40° C) and then reflux 2 hours. Cool, filter and evaporate in vacuum to get the octene, which after catalytic hydrogenation as described for (V) yields (VI).

*5-Alkylresorcinols* Aust. J. Chem. *21*,2979(1968)
Mix 50g 3,5-dihydroxybenzoic acid, 250 g $K_2CO_3$, 200 ml dimethylsulfate and one liter acetone and reflux 4 hours. Remove the acetone, add one liter water and one liter ether to the residue and extract. Wash the ether extract with 2X100 ml concentrated $NH_4OH$, 2X100 ml dilute HCl and 100 ml water and dry, evaporate in vacuum to get 48g methyl-3,5-dimethoxybenzoate (I). Recrystallize from aqueous methanol. To a stirred suspension of 19g lithium aluminium hydride in 200 ml ether add 78.4g (I) in 300 ml ether at a rate which gives gentle refluxing. Reflux 2½ hours, cool and add 50 ml wet ether; then 100 ml dilute sulfuric acid. Wash and dry, evaporate in vacuum the ether extract to get 62g oily 3,5-dimethoxybenzyl alcohol(II). Recrystallize from ether-pentane. To a cooled stirred slurry of 15g $CrO_3$ and 250 ml pyridine add 8.4g (II) in 25 ml pyridine and let stand 1 hour at room temperature. Add 60 ml methanol, let stand 2 hours, and dilute with 500 ml 5% NaOH and 500 ml ether. Extract the aqueous layer with ether and wash the combined ether layers with 500 ml water, 3X500 ml 5% sulfuric

acid, 500 ml water and 200 ml saturated NaCl and dry, evaporate in vacuum to get 7g 3,5-dimethoxybenzaldehyde(III). Recrystallize from ether-pentane. To a flask with a dropping funnel and condenser add 0.58g Mg turnings and 10 ml ether. Add a few drops of a solution of lauryl bromide (5.7g) or equimolar amount of homolog in 15 ml ether and start reaction by adding 2 drops methyl iodide. Add the remaining bromide solution with stirring and gentle refluxing over 15 minutes and then reflux 3 hours. Cool in an ice bath and add 3.1g (III) in 5 ml ether dropwise with stirring over 45 minutes. Reflux 4 hours, cool and dilute with ice water. Wash the organic layer with 2X 25 ml 3N sulfuric acid, 2X25 ml 10% $K_2CO_3$, 25 ml water, 25 ml saturated NaCl and dry, evaporate in vacuum to get 5g 3,5-dimethoxyphenyldodecyl methanol(IV) or homolog. Recrystallize from methanol. Hydrogenate 4.2g (IV) in 50 ml ethyl acetate with 5 drops concentrated sulfuric acid and 0.5g 10% Palladium-Carbon catalyst at room temperature and 5 atmospheres hydrogen for 4 hours. Filter and evaporate in vacuum to get the alkylresorcinol dimethyl ether.

Aust. J. Chem. 26,799(1973) gives a 2 step synthesis of 5-alkylresorcinols by condensation of beta-ketosulphones with 3,5-dimethoxybenzyl bromide and then reduction. Aust. J. Chem. 26,183(1973) gives a synthesis from 3,5-dimethoxy-N,N-dimethylbenzylamine in 7 steps (but perhaps only 4 will reach a cpd. that can give an active THC analog).

*5-Alkylresorcinols* CPB 20,1574(1972)

To a solution of 0.02M ethyl-β-ketocaprylate (or homolog) in 20 ml tetrahydrofuran, add 1.02g (0.02M) (53% oil) NaH with stirring and cooling and then add a solution of diketene (1.68g, 0.02M) in 20 ml tetrahydrofuran dropwise, keeping the temperature between -5 and 0° C. Stir 1 hour at this temperature and then 1 hour at room temperature. Neutralize with 10% HCl and extract with ether. Dry and evaporate in vacuum to get about 38% yield of ethyl-olivetol carboxylate (I). (I) can be purified on silica gel, the impurities being eluted with petroleum ether (30-35° C) and the product with 8:1 petroleum ether:ether. Recrystallize from n-hexane. Dissolve 0.2g (I) in 10 ml 10% NaOH and reflux 30 minutes. Acidify with 10% HCl and extract with ether. Wash the extract with water and dry, evaporate in vacuum (can distill 126–129/3) to get 96% olivetol (or homolog).

For new, simple, high yield syntheses of 5-alkyl resorcinols see TL 4839(1973), 2511(1975) and CJC 52:2136(1974).

# Notes

## Chapter One

1. R. Mechoulam, et al., "Recent Advances in the Chemistry and Biochemistry of *Cannabis*," *Chemical Reviews*, 76 (1976): 75; R. Mechoulam, *Marijuana* (New York: Academic Press, 1973); M. Perez-Reyes, et al., "A Comparison of the Pharmacological Activity in Man of Intravenously Administered $\Delta^9$-Tetrahydrocannabinol, Cannabinol and Cannabidiol," *Experientia* 29 (1973): 1368.
2. I. Karniol, et al., "Cannabidiol Interferes with the Effects of $\Delta^9$ THC in Man," *European Journal of Pharmacology* 28 (1974): 172; I. Karniol, "Effects of $\Delta^9$ THC and Cannabinol in Man," *Pharacology* 13 (1975): 502; L. Hollister, "Cannabidiol and THC Interactions," *Clinical Pharmacology and Therapeutics* 18 (1975): 80.
3. Mechoulam, "Chemistry and Biochemistry of *Cannabis*," 76:75; L.E. Hollister, "Tetrahydrocannabinol Isomers and Homologues: Contrasted Effects of Smoking," *Nature* 227 (1970): 968; G.W. Kinzer et al., "The Fate of the Cannabinoid Components of Marijuana During Smoking," *Bulletin on Narcotics* 26 (1974): 41; A.R. Patel and G.B. Gori, "Preparation and Monitoring of Marijuana Smoke Condensate Samples," *Bulletin on Narcotics* 27 (1975): 47.
4. J.W. Fairbairn et al., "The Stability of *Cannabis* and its Preparations on Storage," *Journal of Pharmacy and Pharmacology* 28 (1976): 1; C.E. Turner et al., "Constituents of *Cannabis Sativa* L. IV: Stability of Cannabinoids in Stored Plant Material," *Journal of Pharmaceutical Science* 62 (1973): 1601.

## Chapter Two

1. R.E. Schultes et al., *"Cannabis:* An Example of Taxonomic Neglect," *Botanical Museum Leaflets, Harvard University* 23 (1974): 337; E. Small, "Interfertility and Chromosomal Uniformity in *Cannabis,"* *Canadian Journal of Botany* 50 (1972): 1947; W.A. Emboden, *"Cannabis*–A Polytypic Genus," *Economic Botany* 28 (1975): 304; E. Small, "American Law and the Species Problem in *Cannabis:* Science and Semantics," *Bulletin on Narcotics* 27 (1975): 1.
2. E. Small, "Morphological Variation of Achemes of *Cannabis,"* *Canadian Journal of Botany* 63 (1975): 978; Emboden, *"Cannabis,"* 28 304; E.H. Toole et al., "Preservation of Hemp and Kenaf Seed," *U.S. Department of Agriculture Technical Bulletin* 1215 (1960).
3. C.T. Hammond and P.G. Mahlberg, "Morphology of Glandular Hairs of *Cannabis Sativa* from Scanning Electron Microscopy," *American Jour-*

*nal of Botany* 60 (1973): 524; A. de Pasquale et al., "Micromorphology of the Epidermic Surfaces of Female Plants of *Cannabis Sativa,*" *Bulletin on Narcotics* 26 (1974): 27.

4. J. Bouquet, "Nouvelle Contributions a l'Etude de la *Cannabis,*" *Archives de la Institute de Pasteur de Tunis* 26 (1937): 288 and 27 (1938): 27.

5. L. Crombie and W. Crombie, "Cannabinoid Formation in *Cannabis Sativa* Grafted Inter-Racially, and With Two Humulus Species," *Phytochemistry* 12 (1975): 409.

6. P. Furst, ed., *Flesh of the Gods* (New York: Praeger, 1972).

7. J. Frazier, *The Marijuana Farmers* (New Orleans: Solar Age Press, 1974).

8. H. Warmke, "Polyploidy Investigations," *Carnegie Institution of Washington Yearbook* (1941), p. 186.

**Chapter Three**

1. K.D. Rasmussen and J.J. Herweijer, "Examination of the Cannabinoids in Young *Cannabis* Plants," *Pharmaceutisch Weekblad* 110 (1975): 91; J.W. Fairbairn and M.G. Rowen, "Cannabinoid Pattern in *Cannabis Sativa* L. Seedlings as an Indication of Chemical Race," *Journal of Pharmacy and Pharmacology,* supplement (1975): 90.

2. E. Small and H.D. Beckstead, "Common Cannabinoid Phenotypes in 350 Stocks of *Cannabis,*" *Lloydia* 36 (1973): 144; E. Small et al., "The Evolution of Cannabinoid Phenotypes in *Cannabis,*" *Economic Botany* 29 (1975): 219; F. Boucher, "Etude Physiologique et Chimique du *Cannabis Sativa* L. Originaire d'Afrique du Sud," Thesis, Curie University, Paris (1976).

3. R. Phillips et al., "Seasonal Variation in Cannabinolic Content of Indiana Marijuana," *Journal of Forensic Science* 15 (1970): 191; A. Haney and B. Kutscheid, "Quantitative Variation in the Chemical Constituents of Marihuana from Stands of Naturalized *Cannabis Sativa* L. in East-Central Illinois," *Economic Botany* 27 (1973): 193 and 29 (1975): 153.

4. M. Paris et al., "The Constituents of *Cannabis Sativa* Pollen," *Economic Botany* 29 (1975): 243; J.W. Fairbairn and J.A. Leibmann, "The Cannabinoid Content of *Cannabis Sativa* L. Grown in England," *Journal of Pharmacy and Pharmacology* 26 (1975): 245; A. Nordal and O. Braenden, "Variations in the Cannabinoid Content of *Cannabis* Plant Grown From the Same Batches of Seeds Under Different Ecological Conditions," *Meddelelser Norsk Farmaceutisk Selskap* 35 (1973): 8; C.B. Coffman and W.A. Gentner, "Cannabinoid Profile and Elemental Uptake of *Cannabis Sativa* L. as Influenced by Soil Characteristics," *Agronomy Journal* 67 (1975): 491; F.A. Bazzaz et al., "Photosynthesis and Cannabinoid Content of Temperate and Tropical Populations of *Cannabis Sativa,*" *Biochemical Systematics and Ecology* 3 (1975): 15; F. Boucher et al., "Le *Cannabis Sativa* L. Races Chemiques ou Varieties," *Plantes Medicinales Phytotherapie* 8 (1974): 20.

**Chapter Four**

1. T. Malingre et al., "The Essential Oil of *Cannabis Sativa,*" *Planta Medica* 28 (1975): 56; M.C. Nigam et al., "Essential Oils and Their Consti-

tuents XXIX," *Canadian Journal of Chemistry* 43 (1965): 3372; L. Martin et al., "Essential Oil From Fresh *Cannabis Sativa* and its Use in Identification," *Nature* 191 (1961): 774.

2. Mobarak et al., "Studies on Non-Cannabinoids of Hashish II," *Chemosphere* 3 (1974): 5.

3. C.E. Turner et al., "Isolation of Cannabisatavine, an Alkaloid From *Cannabis Sativa* L. Root," *Journal of Pharmaceutical Science* 65 (1976): 1084; "The Isolation and Characterization of the Alkaloid Cannabisativine From the Leaves of a Thailand Variant of *Cannabis Sativa* L.," U.N. Secretariat Document ST/SOA/Serv: S/52 (1975); F. Klein and H. Rapoport, "*Cannabis* Alkaloids," *Nature* 232 (1971): 258; Paris, "*Cannabis Sativa* Pollen," p. 245.

4. T.N. Ilinskata and M.G. Yosifova, "Influence of the Conditions Under Which the Poppy is Grown on the Alkaloid Content of the Opium Obtained," *Bulletin on Narcotics* 8 (1956): 38; H.L. Tookey et al., "Effects of Maturity and Plant Spacing on the Morphine Content of Two Varieties of *Popover Somniferum* L.," *Bulletin on Narcotics* 27 (1975): 49.

## Chapter Five

1. J. Bouchet, "*Cannabis,*" *Bulletin on Narcotics* 2 (1950): 14; I.C. Chopra and R.N. Chopra, "The Use of *Cannabis* Drugs in India," *Bulletin on Narcotics* 9 (1957): 4; "Indian Hemp Drugs Commission Report 1893-1894, (7 vols)," U.S. Government Printing Office.

2. Bouquet, "*Cannabis,*" p. 14; Chopra and Chopra, "Use of *Cannabis* in India," p. 4.

3. P. Lys, "Le Chanvre Indien au Liban," *Annales de la Francaise de Medecine et de Pharmacie de Beyrouth* 1 (1932): 333.

4. Chopra and Chopra, "Use of *Cannabis* in India," p. 4.

5. P. Brotteaux, *Hachich* (Paris: Vega, 1934); L. Rosenthaler, "Uber Griechischen Hanf," *Journal de Pharmacie de Alsace-Lorraine* 38 (1911): 232.

## Chapter Seven

1. A. Caldas, "Chemical Identification of *Cannabis,*" *Analytica Chimica Acta* 49 (1970): 194; Z.I. El-Darawy et al., "Studies on Hashish IV Color Reactions of Cannabinols," *Qualitas Plantarum Materiales Vegetabilis* 22 (1972): 7; Anon, "Methods for the Identification of *Cannabis,*" *United Nations Secretariat Document* ST/SOA/Ser. S/1; H.M. Stone, "An Investigation into Forensic Chemical Problems Associated with *Cannabis,*" *United Nations Secretariat Document* ST/SOA/Ser.: 19; L. Grlic, "Peroxide-Sulphuric Acid Test As An Indication of the Ripeness and Physiological Activity of *Cannabis* Resin," *Journal of Pharmacy and Pharmacology* 13 (1961): 637; A. Dronyssion-Asteriou and C.J. Miras, "Fluorescence of Cannabinoids," *Bulletin on Narcotics* 26 (1974): 19.

2. Dronyssion-Asteriou and Miras, "Fluorescence," p. 135; H. de Clercq et al., "Une Reaction d'Identification Fluorimetrique des Constituents du *Cannabis,*" *Journal de Pharmacie Belgique* 28 (1973): 437; M. Hoton-Dorge, "Isolement des Principaux Constiuents Phenoliques du Chanvre Indien, Par Chromotographie Preparative," *Journal de Pharmacie Belgique* 29 (1974): 415.

3. Z.I. El-Darawy et al., "Studies on Hashish III Colorimetric Determination of Cannabinols," *Dissertationes Pharmaceutical et Pharmacological* 24 (1972): 313; M.J. de Faubert Maunder, "An Improved Procedure for the Field Testing of *Cannabis," Bulletin on Narcotics* 26 (1974): 19; C.L. Strong, "Thin Layer Chromatography," *Scientific American* February (1976).

# Glossary

**cyclize**—to form into a circle. Specifically, to link the OH group of CBD to the carbon atom to form the 3 ring compound THC, from the 2 ring compound CBD.

**decarboxylate**—to remove a carboxyl (-COOH) group from a molecule. Specifically, to remove the carboxyl group from THC acid or CBD acid, by heating, to give THC or CBD.

**dioecious**—having the reproductive parts for the two sexes on separate plants.

**genotype**—the genetic makeup or hereditary characteristics of an organism, usually contained in the DNA of the cell nucleus.

**isomerize**—to rearrange the atoms of a molecule such that the molecular weight remains the same but the chemical or physical properties change. Specifically, when CBD is cyclized to THC, it has undergone isomerization.

**monoecious**—having reproductive parts for both sexes on one plant, but in separate flowers for higher plants.

**phenotype**—the observable physical or chemical characteristics of an organism. Color, structure and chemical composition of a plant may all be phenotypic characters.

**polymers**—a complex chemical compound formed of many simpler units. Cellulose is a sugar polymer and gelatin is an amino acid polymer.

**polyploid**—having more than the normal of original number of sets of chromosomes. The cells of most organisms have two sets and are called diploid.

**senescence**—the final stages of the aging of an organism leading to its death.

**synergize**—the working together of two forces or chemicals to produce an effect greater than the sum of their individual effects. Specifically, THC and CBD together may synergize to produce redder eyes than the sum of the redness of the same amounts of the two, taken alone.

# Bibliography

Bazzaz, F.A. et al. "Photosynthesis of Cannabinoid Content of Temperate and Tropical Populations of *Cannabis sativa.*" *Biochemical Systematics and Ecology* 3 (1975): 15.

Boucher, F. "Etude Physiologique et Chimique du *Cannabis sativa* L. Originaire d'Afrique du Sud." Thesis, Curie University, Paris, 1976.

Boucher, F. et al. "Le *Cannabis sativa* L. Races Chemiques ou Varieties." *Plantes Medicinales Phytotherapie* 8 (1974): 20.

Bouchet, J. *"Cannabis." Bulletin on Narcotics* 2 (1950): 14.

Bouquet, J. "Nouvelle Contributions a l'Etude de la *Cannabis." Archives de la Institute de Pasteur de Tunis* 26 (1937): 288, and 27 (1938): 27.

Brotteaux, P. *Hachich.* Paris: Vega, 1934.

Caldas, A. "Chemical Identification of *Cannabis." Analytica Chimica Acta* 49 (1970): 194.

Chopra, I.C., and Chopra, R.N. "The Use of *Cannabis* Drugs in India." *Bulletin on Narcotics* 9 (1957): 4.

Clercq, H. de et al. "Une Reaction d'Identification Fluorimetrique des Constituents de *Cannabis." Journal de Pharmacie Belgique* 28 (1973): 437.

Coffman, C.B., and Gentner, W.A. "Cannabinoid Profile and Elemental Uptake of *Cannabis sativa* L. as Influenced by Soil Characteristics." *Agronomy Journal* 67 (1975): 491.

——— "Effect of Drying Time and Temperature on Cannabinoid Profile of Stored Leaf Tissue." *Bulletin on Narcotics* 26 (1974): 67.

Crombie, L., and Crombie, W. "Cannabinoid Formation in *Cannabis sativa* Grafted Inter-Racially, and With Two Humulus Species." *Phytochemistry* 12 (1975): 409.

Dronyssion-Asterious, A., and Miras, C.J. "Fluorescence of Cannabinoids." *Bulletin on Narcotics* 26 (1974): 19.

El-Darawy, Z.I. et al. "Studies on Hashish III Colorimetric Determination of Cannabinols." *Dissertationes Pharmaceutical et Pharmacological* 24 (1972): 313.

——— "Studies on Hashish IV Color Reactions of Cannabinols." *Qualitas Plantarum Materiales Vegetabilis* 22 (1972): 7.

Emboden, W.A. *"Cannabis*—A Polytypic Genus." *Economic Botany* 28 (1975): 304.

Fairbairn, J.W., and Leibmann, J.A. "The Cannabinoid Content of *Cannabis sativa* L. Grown in England." *Journal of Pharmacy and Pharmacology* 26 (1975): 245.

————, and Rowen, M.G. "Cannabinoid Pattern in *Cannabis sativa* L. Seedlings as an Indication of Chemical Race." *Journal of Pharmacy and Pharmacology,* supplement (1975): 90.

———— et al. "The Stability of *Cannabis* and its Preparations on Storage." *Journal of Pharmacy and Pharmacology* 28 (1976): 1.

Faubert Maunder, M.J. de. "An Improved Procedure for the Field Testing of *Cannabis.*" *Bulletin on Narcotics* 26 (1974): 19.

Frazier, J. *The Marijuana Farmers.* New Orleans: Solar Age Press, 1974.

Furst, P., ed. *Flesh of the Gods.* New York: Praeger, 1972.

Grlic, L. "Peroxide-Sulphuric Acid Test as an Indication of the Ripeness and Physiological Activity of *Cannabis* Resin." *Journal of Pharmacy and Pharmacology* 13 (1961): 637.

Hammond, C.T., and Mahlberg, P.G. "Morphology of Glandular Hairs of *Cannabis sativa* from Scanning Electron Microscopy." *American Journal of Botany* 60 (1973): 524.

Haney, A., and Kutscheid, B. "Quantitative Variation in the Chemical Constituents of Marihuana from Stands of Naturalized *Cannabis sativa* L. in East-Central Illinois." *Economic Botany* 27 (1973): 193, and 29 (1975): 153.

Hanus, L. et al. "Production of $\Delta^9$ Tetrahydrocannabinal from Hemp Cultivated in Climatic Conditions of Czechoslovakia." *Acta Universitatis Palackianae Olomucensis* 74 (1975): 173.

Hollister, L. "Cannabidiol and THC Interactions." *Clinical Pharmacology and Therapeutics* 18 (1975): 80.

Hoten-Dorge, M. "Isolement des Principaux Constituents Phenoliques du Chanvre Indien, Par Chromotographie Preparative." *Journal de Pharmacie Belgique* 29 (1974): 415.

Ilinskata, T.N., and Yosifova, M.G. "Influence of the Conditions Under Which the Poppy is Grown on the Alkaloid Content of the Opium Obtained." *Bulletin on Narcotics* 8 (1956): 38.

"Indian Hemp Drugs Commission Report 1893-1894, (7 vols.)." U.S. Government Printing Office.

Isbell, H. et al. "Effects of (-)$\Delta^9$ Trans-Tetrahydrocannabinol in Man." *Psychopharmacologia* 11 (1967): 184.

"The Isolation and Characterization of the Alkaloid Cannabisativine from the Leaves of a Thailand Variant of *Cannabis sativa* L." United Nations Secretariat Document ST/SOA/Serv: S/52 (1975).

Karniol, I. "Effects of $\Delta^9$ THC and Cannabinol in Man." *Pharmacology* 13 (1975): 502.

———— et al. "Cannabidiol Interferes with the Effects of $\Delta^9$ THC in Man." *European Journal of Pharmacology* 28 (1974): 172.

Kinzer, G.W. et al. "The Fate of the Cannabinoid Components of Marijuana During Smoking." *Bulletin on Narcotics* 26 (1974): 41.

Klein, F., and Rapoport, H. "*Cannabis* Alkaloids." *Nature* 232 (1971): 258.

Krejci, Z. et al. "The Effect of Climatic and Ecologic Conditions Upon the Formation and the Amount of Cannabinoid Substances in *Cannabis* of Various Provenance." *Acta Universitatis Palackianae Olomucensis Facultas Medicae* 74 (1975): 147.

Loev, B. et al. "Cannabinoids: Structure-Activity Studies Related to 1, 2-Dimethylhemtyl Derivatives." *Journal of Medicinal Chemistry* 16 (1973): 1200.

Lys, P. "Le Chanvre Indien au Liban." *Annales de la Francaise de Medecine et de Pharmacie de Beyrouth* 1 (1932): 333.

Malingre, T. et al. "The Essential Oil of *Cannabis sativa*." *Planta Medica* 28 (1975): 56.

Martin, L. et al. "Essential Oil from Fresh *Cannabis sativa* and its Use in Identification." *Nature* 191 (1961): 774.

Mechoulam, R. *Marijuana*. New York: Academic Press, 1973.

—— et al. "Recent Advances in the Chemistry and Biochemistry of *Cannabis*." *Chemical Reviews* 76 (1976): 75.

"Methods for the Identification of *Cannabis*." United Nations Secretariat Document ST/SOA/Serv. S/1.

Miras, C. et al. "Comparative Assay of the Constituents from the Sublimate of Smoked *Cannabis* with that from Ordinary *Cannabis*." *Bulletin on Narcotics* 16 (1964): 13.

Mobarak et al. "Studies on Non-Cannabinoids of Hashish II." *Chemosphere* 3 (1974): 5.

Narayanazwami, K. et al. "Stability of *Cannabis* (Resin) Charas Samples Under Tropical Conditions." *Forensic Science* 5 (1975): P153.

Nigam, M.C. et al. "Essential Oils and Their Constituents XXIX." *Canadian Journal of Chemistry* 43 (1965): 3372.

Nordal, A., and Braenden, O. "Variations in the Cannabinoid Content of *Cannabis* Plant Grown from the Same Batches of Seeds Under Different Ecological Conditions." *Meddelelser Norsk Farmaceutisk Selskap* 35 (1973): 8.

Paris, M. et al. "The Constituents of *Cannabis sativa* Pollen." *Economic Botany* 29 (1975): 243.

Pasquale, A. de. "Farmacognosia della 'Canape Indiana' I." *Lavori dell' Istitute di Farmacognosia dell'Universita di Messina* 5 (1967): 1.

—— et al. "Micromorphology of the Epidermic Surfaces of Female Plants of *Cannabis sativa*." *Bulletin on Narcotics* 26 (1974): 27.

Patel, A.R., and Gori, G.B. "Preparation and Monitoring of Marijuana Smoke Condensate Samples." *Bulletin on Narcotics* 27 (1975): 47.

Perez-Reyes, M. et al. "A Comparison of the Pharmacological Activity in Man of Intraveneously Administered $\Delta^9$ Tetrahydrocannabinol, Cannabinol and Cannabidiol." *Experientia* 29 (1973): 1368.

Phillips. R. et al. "Seasonal Variation in Cannabinolic Content of Indiana Marijuana." *Journal of Forensic Science* 15 (1970): 191.

Quimby, M.W. et al. "Mississippi-Grown Marihuana-*Cannabis sativa* Cultivation and Observed Morphological Variations." *Economic Botany* 27 (1973): 117.

Rasmussen, K.D., and Herweiger, J.J. "Examination of the Cannabinoids in Young *Cannabis* Plants." *Pharmaceutisch Weekblad* 110 (1975): 91.

Rosenthaler, L. "Uber Griechischen Hanf." *Journal de Pharmacie de Alsace-Lorraine* 38 (1911): 232.

Schultes, R.E. et al. *"Cannabis:* An Example of Taxonomic Neglect." *Botanical Museum Leaflets, Harvard University* 23 (1974): 337.

Segelman, A.B., and Sofia, R.D. *"Cannabis sativa* L. (Marijuana) IV: Chemical Basis for Increased Potency Related to Novel Method of Preparation." *Journal of Pharmaceutical Sciences* 62 (1973): 2044.

———— et al. *"Cannabis sativa* L. (Marijuana) V: Pharmacological Evaluation of Marijuana Aqueous Extract and Volatile Oil." *Journal of Pharmaceutical Sciences* 63 (1974): 962.

Shoyama, Y. et al. *"Cannabis* IV. Smoking Test." *Yakugaku Zasshi* 89 (1969): 842.

Small, E. "American Law and the Species Problem in *Cannabis:* Science and Semantics." *Bulletin on Narcotics* 27 (1975): 1.

———— "Interfertility and Chromosomal Uniformity in *Cannabis."* *Canadian Journal of Botany* 50 (1972): 1947.

———— "Morphological Variation of Achemes of *Cannabis."* *Canadian Journal of Botany* 63 (1975): 978.

————, and Beckstead, H.D. "Common Cannabinoid Phenotypes in 350 Stocks of *Cannabis" Lloydia* 36 (1973): 144.

———— et al. "The Evolution of Cannabinoid Phenotypes in *Cannabis."* *Economic Botany* 29 (1975): 219.

Stone, H.M. "An Investigation into Forensic Chemical Problems Associated with *Cannabis." United Nations Secretariat Document ST/SOA/ Serv.:* 19.

Strong, C.L. "Thin Layer Chromatography." *Scientific American* February (1976).

Tookey, H.L. et al. "Effects of Maturity and Plant Spacing on the Morphine Content of Two Varieties of *Popover somniferum* L." *Bulletin on Narcotics* 27 (1975): 49.

Toole, E.H. et al. "Preservation of Hemp and Kenaf Seed." *U.S. Department of Agriculture Technical Bulletin* 1215 (1960).

Turner, C.E. et al. "Constituents of *Cannabis sativa* L. IV: Stability of Cannabinoids in Stored Plant Material." *Journal of Pharmaceutical Science* 62 (1973): 1601.

———— "Isolation of Cannabisatavine, an Alkaloid from *Cannabis sativa* L. Root." *Journal of Pharmaceutical Science* 65 (1976): 1084.

Warmke, H. "Polyploidy Investigations." *Carnegie Institution of Washington Yearbook* (1941): 186.

Zeeuw, R.A. de et al. "$\Delta^1$-Tetrahydrocannabinolic Acid, an Important Component in the Evaluation of *Cannabis* Products." *Journal of Pharmacy and Pharmacology* 24 (1972): 1.

# Marijuana Chemistry Update
(Page numbers indicate placement of update in original edition)


page 5

A new compound, $\Delta^7$-cis-iso-tetrahydrocannabivarin, has been isolated from Thai marijuana (CPB 29, 3720 [1981]). For the biosynthesis of propyl and other cannabinoids see Phyto-chemistry 23, 1909 (1984). Further evidence that CBN and CBN acid are aging products is given by Acta Univ. Palacki Olomuc Fac. Med. 108, 29 (1985).


page 6

A study of Sadhus (holy men) in India who smoked ganja daily an average of eleven years found little or no obvious harm (Quarterly J. Crude Drug Res. 19 (2), 81 (1981).


page 10

In evaluating cannabinoid activity it should be noted that psychoactive drugs often have complex wavelike activity with multiple effects that wax and wane.


page 10

Some good work on the relationships between the high, peak blood levels and potency of reefer have appeared in Clin.

Pharmacol. Therap. 31, 617 (1982) and Psychopharmacology 75, 158 (1981). It has been shown (by Brazilian researchers!) that when CBD is present in twice the amount of THC, it decreases the anxiety and some other effects of THC but does not block the pulse rate increase and produces some effects opposite to those of THC [Psychopharmacology 76, 245 (1982): see also 80, 325 (1983)].

page 12
Experiments with an automatic smoking machine showed 62 percent of the THC and THCA appearing in the tar and 2 percent in the ash with the rest destroyed [(J. Anal. Toxicol. 9, 121 (1985). The basic fraction of the smoke condensate has little activity in mice (Toxicol Appl. Pharm. 72, 440 (1984).]

page 12
A recent study [Clinical Pharmacol. Therap. 28, 409 (1980)] found that about 18 percent of the THC smoked appeared in the blood versus only 6 percent of that eaten. However, the situation is more complex since eating produced effects at much lower blood levels than smoking or injection.

page 15
A recent study of THC oil mixed in marijuana found that only storage in a freezer at minus 18 degrees centigrade prevented rapid degeneration. Storing in a refrigerator at 5 degrees centigrade, at room temperature under nitrogen, or at room temperature in the dark all led to decomposition of about 75 percent of the THC in twelve weeks. (J. P. S. 67, 876 (1978)).

page 17
The morphology of Brazilian hemp is described in Rev.
Cienc. Farm 4, 31 (1982). The morphology and cannabinoids
of Egyptian plants are presented in Biological Abstracts 76 (2)
#8474.

page 18
Crosses between *C. ruderalis* and *C. sativa* [Econ. Bot. 32, 387
(1978)] are intermediate in most characters, but they have
either high or low THC. Also, a careful study of twenty wild
*C. sativa* strains in India and their seeds grown in the U.S. has
appeared (see note for page 85).
Line 8 should read "stainable".

page 19
The figure shown here has been reversed in printing and the
fiber variant is found on the right. Emboden [J Psychoactive
Drugs 13, 15, (81)] has forcefully stated the case for polyspeci-
fic nature of the genus *Cannabis*. I agree completely.

page 20
An analysis of the constituents of ten varieties of hemp seeds
led to the conclusion that there was only one species (Biological Abstracts 76, #62453).

page 22
A study of wild Indian plants showed more glandular
trichomes and more cannabinoids in plants from warm, dry
and windy locations and at lower elevations [Planta Medica
37, 219 (1979)].

page 24
Nearly all the cannabinoids are found in the secretory sac
above the capitate disc of the secretory cells [Botanical Gazette
142, 316 (1981)].
Much work has been done on *Cannabis* glandular hairs. See
Amer. J. Bot. 67, 1397 (1980) and references therein, and
Bulletin on Narcotics 33, (3) 63 (1981). For the THC content of
bracts, see Bulletin on Narcotics 33, (2) 59 (1981). A careful
study of seedlings showed the first appearance of THC at 66
hours [Bot. Gaz. 148 , 468 (87)]

page 25
The legends for figures 10 and 11 have been reversed.

page 29
In at least some plants drastic pruning or grafting or spraying
with a combination of benzyladenine and alphanapthalene
acetic acid will prevent senescence in spite of fruiting [Nature
271, 354 (1978)].

page 31
For more recent cloning studies see Physiologie Vegetale 18,
207–221 (1980) and Planta Med. Phytother. 20 , 99 (86) .

page 33
Plants grown under various filtered lights show less THC
than for daylight conditions [Botanical Gazette 144, 43 (1983)].
For tissue culture see Z. Pflanzenphysiologie 111, 395 (1983),
and Agronomie (Paris) 6 , 487 (86) for tissue culture and clone
preparation.

page 37
A more recent study [Il Farmaco. Ed. Sci. 34, 841–53 (1979)] has shown that some polyploid plants (produced by treating young plants with 0.5 percent colchicine) can have about twice the THC concentration of untreated plants but total yield per plant is probably less. This, coupled with the facts that many plants die, that higher potency plants will probably not breed true and that colchicine is poisonous make it doubtful that such treatment is worth the effort. For further discussion see Clarke's excellent *Marijuana Botany* (And/Or Press, 1981). For a recent Russian paper on the botany of hemp polyploids see Genetika (English Edition) 15, 204 (1979).

page 45
A report [J. Natural Products 42, 317 (1979)] on the extensive studies at the University of Mississippi shows enormous and nearly random variations in the cannabinoid content during weeks 19 to 25 of growth and deduces that it is impossible to simply classify cannabinoid variants. However, like most studies this one did not sample the same individual plants with time but sampled several plants and pooled the results. In view of the tremendous differences between plants from the same batch of seeds, we will have to await further studies of cannabinoid variation in single plants and in clones where the entire cannabinoid content of the plant can be measured during growth, thus minimizing the spurious fluctuations due to changes in other constituents.

page 46
It should be noted that significant amounts of both cannabigerol (India, South Africa) and THCV (India, Sudan, Afghani-

stan, Pakistan, Lebanon) have been shown to occur more widely and all phenothypes are less well-defined geographically than was originally thought. For THCV in Russian marijuana see BA 85, 26311 (87). A cannabigerol dominant type low in THC has been described [Planta Med. 43, 277 (87)]

page 48
A recent study of Mexican and Japanese strains grown in Japan showed no difference between the cannabinoid contents of the sexes. The following data on the appearance and thin layer chromatography of marijuana smuggled into Britain show that it is possible to get a fairly good idea of its origin if all facts are considered.

page 58
Medium and low THC strains of monoecious fiber hemp cultivated in France showed approximately parallel changes in CBD and THC during growth [Physiologia Vegetale 18, 349 (1980)]
It has been claimed [Lloydia 36,144 (1973)] that the sexes are about equal in cannabinoid content in plants originating north of latitude 30 deg N while females are more potent in strains originating south of 30 deg N.
A study of five monoecious fiber strains grown in France showed two cannabinoid types: one with 0.34% THC and 0.63% CBD and one with 0.02% THC and 0.86% CBD [Plantes Medicinales et Phytotherapie 13, 116-121(1979)].
All three strains grown outdoors in Naples gave maximum THC at 25% of full sunlight for both males and females: BA 84 , 94197 (87). Twenty generations of clones of two South African varieties showed constant chemical phenotypes with

cool temperatues best for flowering and hot for growth. Native Sudanese strains have THC but almost no CBD while high CBD strains from Britain showed increased THC and lowered CBD in the first generation in the Sudan [Fitoterapia 57, 165, 239 (86)] . For an update on Czech cannabinoid studies see Acta Univ. Palacki Olomuc. Fac. Med. 114, 11 (86) , 116, 15, 31 (87). The second paper describes cannabinoids in roots.


page 60
Cannabinoid content of hashish and marijuana seized in Sweden: Arch. Kriminol 174,167(1984); content of 39 slabs of Moroccan hash: J. Anal Toxicol 7,7(1983); content of 61 slabs of Lebanese hash (which showed you could tell the batch by cannabinoid profile): J. Chromatographic Sci. 22, 282(1984). See also Forensic Sci 11,189(1978).


page 68
The cannabinoid content of different organs of various strains is given in J. Nat. Prods. 43,112(1980). It is shown that a single flowering top may contain one organ with high THC, low CBD and another with high CBD, low THC. Also, seeds and pollen are shown to contain no cannabinoids (though they are usually contaminated with glandular hairs from the bracts. A recent study of Japanese plants showed that young leaves from anywhere on the plant had a higher percent THC than older leaves [CPB 28,594 (1980)]). More details on the cannabinoid content of South African plants are given in J. Pharm. Pharmacol. 32,21(1980). Small amounts are present in roots [BA 85, 26314 (87)] BA 83, 17922 (87) follows variation with vege-

tative growth.

page 69
In a given African strain, you can tell the propyl THC
types by their longer internodes but the total concentration
of THC was still greater than that of THCV and the highest
THC was in males grown in the 22 degree – 12 degree
phytotron. Cool temperatures produced more intensive
flowering but decreased growth and development [Physi-
ologie Vegetale 18,207(1980)].

page 69
A recent study on South African plants [J. Pharmacy
Pharmacol. 32,21(1980)] found three more or less distinct
cannabinoid phenotypes. The first type, typified by plants
from the Transkei district, had several percent pentyl THC
and virtually no propyl THC. The second type, typified by
plants from Pongola district, had approximately equal
quantities of pentyl and propyl THC during vegetative
growth, but with maturation, both males and females
increased propyl THC to two to three times the pentyl
THC. The third type, typified by plants from Tzaneen
district, contained several times more pentyl THC when
young but by six to twelve weeks the males had about
three times and the females about thirty times more pentyl
than propyl THC. By the time these latter females had
aged three to six months, they matched the males with
about three times more pentyl.

page 72
Several studies have analyzed the cannabinoids of mari-

juana seized in Europe in order to determine potency and its probable country of origin. J. Forensic Sci. Soc. analyzes 242 reefers containing from 6 to 1090 mg of resin which were seized in England and Bulletin on Narcotics 32(4), 47(1980) and 34(3)101(1982) reports on more British seizures. Analusis 13,111(1985) tries to determine origin using gas chromatography and IR spectra, while J. Forensic Sci. Soc. 26(1),35(1986) strives to elucidate origin by the dead insects included. See Bull. on Narcs. 32(4),55(1980) for Italian seizures.


page 81
Herba Hung 23,(12)95(1984) found that the THC/CBD ratio depended on photoperiod and monoecious-dioecious crosses often gave a low THC content. Botanical Gazette 146,32(1985) found random cannabinoid fluctuations through two years in three clones, but all cannabinoids increased or decreased simultaneously with no correlation between the three clones. Morphology and cannabinoid profile were constant. Once again this shows the dominance of genetics and the fallacy of those studies which purport to show dramatic variations of cannabinoid profile with environment. Of course, there may be strains in which cannabinoids do vary with environment but only cloning studies are relevant and they have so far failed to reveal such strains.

A study of plants grown for four generations in England from tropical seeds showed varying total yields from year to year but total THC contents comparable to those of the first generation. THCV levels declined in plants from Southern Africa and rose in many from Morocco and Sri Lanka. Moroccan plants also tended to show increased CBD (Bulletin on Narcotics 37 (4), 75 (85). A recent Study BON 34 (1), 45 (82) from the long Mississippi series compared seven strains grown in Mexico (native) and in Mississippi. The THC varied from 0.14 to 2.97 with 1.69 percent average in Mexico, with only one plant having more than traces of CBD. The Mexican plants grown in the U.S.A. in 1974 had less THC than the plants grown in 1976 leading to the suggestion that lower rainfall and tempera- ture in 1976 were responsible, but once again I must point out that only cloning experiments could prove this and they have always led to the opposite conclusion. For in- stance, the study above (Botanical Gazette 146,32(1985)) of three clones cultivated for two years showed random (rather than cyclic) fluctuations in cannabinoid levels occurring independently from clone to clone. If environ- ment were significant, fluctuations should have been simultaneous for all clones and for all plants within each clone —contrary to observations. See also the phenotypic constancy of clones over 20 generations in Planta Med. Phytother. 20 , 99 (86).

## Mean values of total THC content of plants grown in England

| Country of origin | Seedstock | 1980 | 1981 | 1982 | 1983 |
|---|---|---|---|---|---|
| Morocco | 1.5 | 3.0 | 0.67 | 1.1 | 0.9 |
| Sri Lanka | 1.0 | 1.1 | 0.80 | 1.5 | 2.2 |
| Zambia | 1.5 | 0.84 | 0.73 | 1.6 | 1.2 |

Bulletin on Narcotics, 37(4),75(1985)

page 81

For an analysis of Jamaican marijuana see West Indian Med. J. 34,8(1985). For the content of plants from seeds from all over grown in Hungary see Herba Hung. 19(1),95(1980) and 23,(12),95(1984). The THC content of plants grown on the Danish island of Bornholm ranged from 0.1 to 4.2 percent with an average of 1.55 percent (Bulletin of Narcotics 37(4),87(1985)). When seven Italian strains were grown in maritime, insular or continental sites in Italy, the cannabinoid profiles varied considerably with site, sex and plant part, with the highest THC content in the continental site (Fitoterapia 54,195,237(1983)). Of course, the seeds which grew in one site may not have grown at all in the other sites and only cloning can control for this. Another Italian study followed 176 plants for CBD and THC weekly to conclude that you can tell drug or fiber type from the content of the young plant (Forensic Sci Int 24,37(1984)). Two related Italian studies are Bulletin on Narcotics 37(4),61,67(1985). Data on twenty wild Indian strains and their progeny grown in Mississippi are given in Planta Medica 37, 217(1979).

page 85

A Brazilian study has shown an increase of THC from 1.3 to 2.9 percent in two months when light was increased from ten to twelve hours per day. Bulletin on Narcotics 30,67(1978).

An analysis of twenty wild strains growing in India showed that higher concentrations of cannabinoids and more glandular hairs were found in plants in warm, dry, windy places and at lower elevations (Planta Medica

37,219(1979). When seeds from these wild plants were grown in Mississippi, the plants were about twice as tall and had two to three times as many leaflets per leaf and less variation in total cannabinoid content than their wild Indian parents, but the size of the reproductive parts was about equal. Undoubtedly, natural selection was already at work and definitive studies will require cloning or complete genotyping.

page 85
A recent phytotron (growth chamber) study (Physiol. Vegetale 18,207(1980)) of cloned high propyl THC (THCV) and high pentyl THC types found that growth at 22 degrees C slightly increased the THC concentration, especially in males, whereas 32 degrees C slightly increased THCV concentration, especially in females. The difference was only about 25 percent. It was also found that flowering was stimulated and total growth decreased at 22 degrees relative to 32 degrees. As usual, the total content of cannabinoids was not given.

page 86
Crosses between *Cannabis ruderalis* and *Cannabis sativa* give plants with either high or low THC, but other characteristics are intermediate (Econ Bot 32,387(1978)). Crosses between two different cannabinoid types of Japanese fiber hemp over four generations give first generation plants with cannabinoids of both parents (C.A. 93:91883z(1980)).

There has been some interest in crossing early flowering *C. ruderalis* with *C. sativa* or *C. indica* to get potent strains that will yield a crop in northern latitudes or will give several crops indoors (e. g. see *High Times* p 65 Nov. 1987). This is almost certainly a bad idea. Ruderalis is usually a small plant with little THC and attempts to separate its early flowering from its undesirable characteristics have not and are not likely to be successful. Selgnij and Clarke (*Best of High Times* Vol 6 p14) have stated the situation admirably. In their years of experience, numerous backcrossings of the hybrids with *sativa-indica* stocks have continued to give less potent, lower yielding plants. The spread of ruderalis genes through U.S. sativa-indica stocks is likely to be a disaster. They also claim that the spread of indica genes though U.S. hemp has also decreased potency, flavor and varieties of high, beginning in the 70's when U.S. growers began extensively crossing the earlier flowering indica with sativa. It should be kept in mind that there is plenty of genetic variability in all marijuana and one could try to breed an early flowering variety of sativa just by picking out those plants which flower early. It should also be noted that there is likely to be considerable variety in the seeds from a single plant and that natural selection tends to force genetic change regardless of the grower's desires. Even indoors, the precise conditions of soil, moisture and temperature and light during each day and during the season are very different from those in the high plains of Afghanistan or the lowlands of Thailand. Very recent experiments have shown that genes can change in response to environment. Though these observations have so far been made only in simple organisms, it would not be at all surprising to see them extended to more complex ones.

page 90
A qualitative study of flavonoid variations in marijuana
has recently appeared (Bot J Linnean Soc 79,249(1979)). A
further study of cannabis volatiles has appeared (J. Forensic Sci Soc 26 (1)35(1986)).


page 111
While any of the solvents indicated will extract the cannabinoids with high efficiency, the solvent of choice for
preparing *oil* is hexane or a mixture of hexanes or if un-
available then cyclohexane. These are very nonpolar and
follow the general principle of using the poorest solvent
possible, thus leaving most undesired substances behind.
One of the other less expensive and easier to obtain solvents can first be used to do the extraction and can then be
in turn extracted by repeated washing with hexane and the
hexane then separated and evaporated to yield the oil.
Also, the other solvent could first be evaporated and the
gummy residue then extracted with hexane. Petroleum
ether is an excellent substitute for hexane (diethyl ether is
*not* the same as petroleum ether and is much more danger-
ous to use). To get a highly pure oil, distillation with collection of the THC at about 200 degrees C in a vacuum of
about 0.05 mm Hg is required.


page 113
A fast, efficient high yield oil extraction apparatus called
the "Honeybee" appeared. The small version ($500) does
one pound of marijuana in one hour and the large version
($750) does five pounds. The apparatus is airtight, saving
lungs and solvent. It is also useful for extracting oils from

other plant materials for perfumes, flavorings etc. I have
seen it used and it does perform as advertised. See High
Times Magazine for availability of this and similar devices.

page 127
Bulletin on Narcotics 37(4),83(1985) gives a new tlc method
for cannabinoids.
Bulletin on Narcotics 34(3),109(1982) gives new spot tests.
See also J. Chromatography 171,509(1979).

page 128
For a new colorimetric assay with fast blue BB salt see CA
93,80119d(1980). For new spot tests see BON
34(3),109(1982) and Planta Medica (Suppl)163 (1980).

page 136
When thinking about structure-activity relationships, keep
in mind the crude and preliminary nature of most of the
data and the complex nature of cannabinoid actions. As
discussed earlier, CBD has complex effects on the THC
high and both decreases and prolongs the high and its
effects on the experience may vary dramaticaly for different people. Also, cannabinoids with little psychoactivity
often have other interesting biological actions such as
antinausea, antiglaucoma, antibiotic, hormonal inhibitory,
etc. See "Cannabinoids as Therapeutic Agents" R. Mechoulam (ed) CRC Press (1986).. Aryl and aryloxy substituents
at five prime decrease activity.
S-3-OH-Δ⁹THC is considerably more potent than the R
isomer.

page 138

For excellent recent reviews of cannabinoid chemistry see
The Total Synthesis of Natural Products Vol. 4, 1981 and
J.Nat. Prods. 43,169(1980). For a new, high yield synthesis
of THC as well as an improvement on the BF3-citral
method see JCS Perkin Trans. 1(1),201(1979). Other recent
papers on THC synthesis are JOC 45,751(1980),
44,677(1979); Acta Pharm. Suec. 16,23(1979); JMC
23,1068(1980); Indian J Chem 16B,1112(1978),
17B,250(1979); TET 34,1985(1978); TL 4773(1979); Angew
Chem. 92,130(1980).

THC analogs and derivatives: CJC 60,308(1982); JMC
28,783(1985); CJC 63,632(1985) N analogs: J. Het. Chem
18,23(1981). For 41 percent THC yield with high pressure
see Z. Naturforsch. B 36,275 (1981). For the synthesis of
Δ9cis and trans THC see Aust. J. Chem. 37,2339(1984). For
analogs see JCS Perkin Trans. 1,2881(1984),
2873(1983),2867(1983),2825(1981), 729(1984), HCA 67,1233
(1984), J. Het. Chem 21,121(1984), HCA 63,2508 (1980),
66,2564 (1983), J. Med Chem 25,1447(1982), Arch Pharm
(Weinheim) 315,551(1982). For a simple synthesis of a
potent analog see J. Pharmacol Exptl Ther 223, 516(1982).
For N-propyl and methyl homologs of Δ8 and Δ9 THC
see Biomed. Environmen. Mass Spectrom. 15 , 389, 403 (88).
For n-butyl Δ8 and Δ9 THC see Xenobiotica 18, 417 (88).
for THC analogs see Mol. Pharmacology 33 , 297 (88).  N-
heteroatomic cannabinol analogs Heterocycles (Tokyo) 24,
2831 (86).

The best recent reference on the SAR is Structure Activity Relationships of the Cannabinoids edited by R. Rapaka-NIDA Research Monograph 79 (1987) published by the National Institute on Drug Abuse. Especially interesting is the article on nonclassical compounds by Melvin and Johnson.

page 140
The first method at the top of the page is method 3 for producing the optically active natural isomer and all of the following methods give racemic THC.

page 145
For an alternate route from limonene in about 50 percent yield see Aust. J. Chem. 33,451(1980).

page 163
For new syntheses of olivetol and analogs see JOC 42,3456(1977), 44,4508(1979), and Indian J. Chem. 16B,970(1978).

page 171
A superb review (R. Clarke —*Marijuana Botany*, And/Or Press, 1981) has appeared. However, the statement on page 94 that cannabinoid levels are environmentally determined is wrong or confused and the assertion that males usually have the same ratios in lower amounts than females is subject to many qualifications.

Tips on Cloning and Home Growing from an Old Western Gardener

Dear Sir:

I grow only a few plants for my own use and have done so for the past eight years. I am retired on social security and couldn't afford to smoke if I did not grow my own. I grow my plants organically — horse manure and lime are the only things I put on the ground. I have had outstanding success. I haul horse manure in the summer when it is dry — put in a pile until fall and then spread it about a foot deep over the ground. I don't spade or anything —just make sure there are plenty of night crawlers in it. I start seedlings in the house the first of March and plant them outside 15 April. These I let bloom in the fall for winter smoking. For summer smoking I keep about three female clones through the winter — plant them in the garden the first of April. I find that from May through August the tips of these clones are very good. I keep them low and bushy — 12 to 14 growing tips on each plant. I have found that July and August is the best time to root clones. I keep them short and put them in a south window in the fall. I give them no extra light — just the natural winter sunlight. They are back to producing one petal to a leaf by Christmas time. Four months later they are potent enough to smoke so I have fresh smoking by the first of May. In May they are growing fast enough so you can harvest these tips once a week.

          I believe that new grass is better than old. A friend of mine gave me a sample from plants that were nine months old. He harvested the complete plant and mixed it all together. It made you drunk and dizzy but not high. The next day I felt horrible. By smoking the growing tips after the plant is four months old I've found you have good potency and for about three days you feel like a new man. By summer time the potency is strong enough to give you hallucinations — you feel like you can fly — your eyes dilate — the colors seem to jump right out at you. It quickens the mind and the senses, it relaxes you and you get a feeling of happiness. I've been to the garden of Eden, flew through the universe, saw the most fantastic and beautiful architecture you ever could imagine.

I sample my plants at four months by taking off a tip and smoking it. I air dry these as slowly as possible and never sun dry them. I smoke them with tobacco. When my plants are producing good potency tips faster than I can smoke them, I dry them, put them in plastic bread wrappers and put them in the freezer. I don't crush them, I leave the stem intact until I smoke them. In the fall I harvest only the blooms and the new growth that accompanies them. I smoke no fan leaves except the immature tips. I don't stress my plants in any way. This year I started one plant in January, one in February, and the rest in March. I want to see if the potency starts at four months at the tips in the seedlings as it does in the clones. I set them all out April 15 — that is when the temperature reaches 65 degrees days here in the Willameth valley and the last frost is over. I have been growing it eight years. The first year about eight inches was as high as they got — now they grow eight feet.

By the way, the seed was planted in June 1977 for my clones and I clone them every July or August since then. I've found once they bloom they are hard to root. In July my success ratio was four out of five shoots. This year I tried something different. I laid one of the clones down flat on the ground when I planted it and covered all but the growing tips with sand. If it reverses when it roots, it will be four months before it will be potent enough to smoke. Otherwise, I will have about a dozen clones that I can transplant that I know are females. You have to color code the clones when you clone in July because you can't tell males from females. I clone about a dozen, pick out the three healthiest looking females from the most potent plants and throw the rest away. I put the shoots in Vigro root stimulant for about a week and a half or until I see white bumps forming on the stem. Then I just stick them in well-rotted horse manure. I keep them in the shade the first month or more. I clip them back to sixteen inches high and fourteen inches wide. I do this whenever they are getting too big. The stalk is about 1/2 inch in diameter when I transplant them in spring outdoors. I use a two-gallon pot for each plant when they are in the house. What's nice about these clones is you have fresh smoking when other people are just planting their seed and the ripoff artists never get active until about August or September up here.

I'm so sold on my own plants I won't even sample anybody else's. I smoke about a cigarette every three days with tobacco in a pipe. Other than the taste it's no different than pipe tobacco. I mean by this I don't choke, cough and my eyes water, turn red in the faace and look like I'm dying. About ten minutes after I smoke it, my muscles relax, my eyes dilate, and the high begins. It comes on gradually. I've never timed it but I would say it lasts from fifteen to twenty minutes. The after effects are what is amazing. Before I started smoking it I had leg cramps almost every night. Now I don't have leg cramps at all if I smoke it every three days. Also, I have a lot more energy and don't get tired so easily. For people over fifty years of age I would say it is the fountain of youth.

Almost every animal I know eats it. When I harvest some young tips my two dogs jump all over me until I give them a little bit. Good luck on your book and I hope we can legally grow it soon.

**Marijuana Chemistry Update**

Common visual features of *Cannabis* and cannabis resin
imported into the United Kingdom

| Country | Number of samples examined[a] | Features |
|---------|-------------------------------|----------|
| | | **A.  Cannabis** |
| Ghana | 120 | Brown; often compressed into blocks or slabs; usually leafy with few identifiable flowering or fruiting tops |
| India | 20 | Brown with clumped resinous tops – typical *Cannabis indica;* dark green-brown and chopped or very immature green female plants (three varieties) |
| Jamaica | 350 | Brown and very coarse with a high percentage of stalk and seed; some recent samples as compressed blocks |
| Kenya | 100 | Green or brown material |
| Morocco | 25 | Light green to yellow green and very finely chopped; no recognizable seed or stalk |
| Nigeria | 190 | Brown with small, characteristically twisted stems; often as small pieces rather than whole (fruiting) tops; some recent samples as compressed blocks |
| South Africa | 60 | Green; often in small rolls in brown paper (this variety is usually immature); brown mature (fruiting) variety also occurs |
| Thailand | 110 | Green or brown sticks of several seedless tops tied around bamboo [45] with a number of sticks compressed into a slab; some recent seizures have been loose herb and/or of lower quality [49] |
| Zambia | 40 | Green or brown material; the compressed "corn-cob" shape wrapped in coarse vegetable fibre is characteristic |
| | | **B.  Cannabis resin** |
| India | 120 | Dark-brown, as sticks (often in bundles), balls and irregular shapes and (rarely) as pale-brown "twists"; often mouldy; sometimes encountered as wafers with a glossy surface |
| Lebanon | 100 | Red-brown and powdery, a darker resin than Moroccan; as blocks (often 500 g) in white cotton bags with many different, often crudely made, ink stamps; resin bears imprint of cloth when unwrapped |
| Morocco | 95 | Yellow-brown and powdery in thin, rectangular slabs, wrapped in clear plastic; markings are rare, but include "12 Madeleines" and "6 Madeleines" and coin imprints; biscuity smell when fresh |
| Nepal | 50 | Dark-brown to black in colour; occasionally as large "Temple Balls" but more often as rough lumps (resembling dry soil) or thin, roughly prepared slabs in plastic; often mouldy with almost a perfumed smell and crumbles readily |
| Pakistan | 250 | Dense, dark-brown rectangular or square slabs with a greener interior; pliable with a pleasant smell when fresh, becoming hard, brittle and odourless with age; embossed marks on the resin in various languages or symbols [50] |
| Turkey | 10 | Usually as greenish-brown powder or (rarely) as small thin wafers of brittle material wrapped in thin plastic |

[a]Original seizures of *Cannabis* varied from 100 g to 1,000 kg.

## CHROMATOGRAPHIC FEATURES OF CANNABIS
## ILLEGALLY IMPORTED INTO BRITAIN

| Country | Number of samples examined | TLC features |
|---------|---------|---------|
| | | **A. Cannabis** |
| Ghana | 50 | Very little chemical difference; all lack CBD and have low |
| Jamaica | 150 | THV:THC ratios. Ghana often shows both CBG and CBCh > THV, |
| Nigeria | 100 | while Jamaica and Nigeria usually show THV > both CBG and CBCh |
| India | 10 | "Clumped" variety contains CBD and THC:THV ≅ 1. Green-brown variety resembles Ghana, Jamaica, Nigeria group (no CBD). Immature variety contains CBD. THC:THV ≅ 1, but is very weak in cannabinoid content |
| Kenya | 25 | Both show two varieties, neither having CBD. One has THC:THV ≅ 1 |
| Zambia | 10 | with low CBG and CBCh. The other variety resembles the Ghana, Jamaica, Nigeria group |
| Morocco | 10 | TLC pattern identical to Moroccan cannabis resin |
| South Africa | 20 | No CBD. Greenish varieties sometimes show THC:THV ≅ 1. More usually, the TLC is similar to the Ghana, Jamaica, Nigeria group. A few samples have an unidentified orange spot with $R_f$ similar to THV |
| Thailand | 25 | Normally only THC and THC acid. No CBD and negligible THV |
| | | **B. Cannabis resin** |
| India | 35 | Very variable. CBD:THC may vary from unity to very small CBG and CBCh ≅ THV ⩽ THC |
| Lebanon | 25 | CBD > THC<br>THV is very low<br>Acids may be high and grossly overload the TLC plate, running as a yellow streak |
| Morocco | 15 | CBD:THC ≅ 1:2<br>THV is low<br>CBG and CBCh > THV<br>A yellow spot $R_f$ ≅ 0.9 is often noted before spraying<br>The amount of cannabinoid acids is variable, appearing as a yellow streak after spraying |
| Nepal | 20 | CBD may be very low and almost absent<br>THC > THV ≅ CBG and CBCh |
| Pakistan | 100 | A similar pattern to Morocco sample, but the cannabinoid acids are less marked<br>CBG and CBCh > THV (fresh samples are very rare) |
| Turkey | 5 | CBD:THC ≅ 1:4<br>CBG and CBCh > THV<br>Cannabinoid acids may be very high and seriously distort the TLC pattern, yellow streaking running to $R_f$ ≅ 0.5 or more |

## Total THC content of seized cannabis

| Country or area of origin | 1975 Number of samples | 1975 THC content (%) Range | 1975 THC content (%) Mean | 1976 Number of samples | 1976 THC content (%) Range | 1976 THC content (%) Mean | 1978 Number of samples | 1978 THC content (%) Range | 1978 THC content (%) Mean |
|---|---|---|---|---|---|---|---|---|---|
| Bangladesh | 5 | 1.4- 4.4 | 3.0 | – | | | – | | |
| Colombia | – | | | – | | | 3 | 2.5- 3.9 | 3.4 |
| Ghana | 7 | 0.7- 2.5 | 1.6 | 9 | 0.4- 2.8 | 1.3 | 6 | 1.4- 3.4 | 2.4 |
| India | – | | | 1 | 2.7 | 2.7 | 4 | 1.7- 7.8 | 5.5 |
| Jamaica | 16 | 0.2- 2.7 | 1.8 | 9 | 0.7- 3.3 | 1.9 | 15 | 1.5- 5.0 | 3.7 |
| Kenya | 1 | 2.7 | 2.7 | 6 | 1.0- 4.2 | 2.2 | 13 | 1.0- 3.9 | 2.2 |
| Morocco | – | | | – | | | 2 | 0.9- 1.3 | 1.1 |
| Nigeria | 2 | 2.0- 2.8 | 2.4 | 5 | 0.8- 5.9 | 3.4 | 16 | 2.3- 7.4 | 4.1 |
| South Africa | 5 | 2.3- 6.3 | 4.1 | 5 | 0.6- 2.8 | 2.6 | 8 | 2.3- 5.5 | 3.6 |
| Southern Rhodesia | – | | | – | | | 2 | 2.7-12 | 7.3 |
| Swaziland | 2 | 2.1- 2.4 | 2.3 | – | | | – | | |
| Thailand | 10 | 3.8-17 | 7.8 | 11 | 5.1-17 | 9.3 | 13 | 0.4- 8.8 | 3.9 |
| Zambia | 2 | 2.2- 2.7 | 2.5 | 4 | 2.6- 4.1 | 3.9 | 4 | 1.3- 4.0 | 2.3 |
| Total | 50 | | | 50 | | | 86 | | |

## Total THC content of seized cannabis resin

| Country of origin | 1975 Number of samples | 1975 THC content (%) Range | 1975 THC content (%) Mean | 1976 Number of samples | 1976 THC content (%) Range | 1976 THC content (%) Mean | 1978 Number of samples | 1978 THC content (%) Range | 1978 THC content (%) Mean |
|---|---|---|---|---|---|---|---|---|---|
| India | – | | | 1 | 3.5 | 3.5 | 11 | 2.2-26 | 11 |
| Iran | 2 | 1.5- 2.7 | 2.1 | – | | | – | | |
| Lebanon | – | | | 10 | 2.2- 8.0 | 4.4 | 3 | 1.0- 8.5 | 4.3 |
| Morocco | 6 | 4.0-16 | 9.5 | 2 | 3.8- 9.4 | 6.6 | 7 | 4.7- 9.2 | 7.4 |
| Nepal | – | | | 2 | 14 | 14 | 2 | 11 | 11 |
| Pakistan | 3 | 2.5- 7.3 | 4.6 | 5 | 3.9-12 | 7.2 | 19 | 3.2-16 | 6.2 |
| Turkey | – | | | – | | | 4 | 8.8-13 | 10 |
| Total | 11 | | | 20 | | | 46 | | |

## Total THC content of seized "hash oil"

| Country of origin | 1977 Number of samples | 1977 THC content (%) Range | 1977 THC content (%) Mean | 1978 Number of samples | 1978 THC content (%) Range | 1978 THC content (%) Mean |
|---|---|---|---|---|---|---|
| India | 5 | 20-48 | 33 | 1 | 40 | 40 |
| Kenya | 2 | 28-39 | 34 | – | | |
| Lebanon | – | | | 2 | 16 | 16 |
| Morocco | – | | | 8 | 2-18 | 8.5 |
| Pakistan | 12 | 25-42 | 30 | 11 | 13-29 | 18 |
| Total | 19 | | | 22 | | |

## Total THC content of cannabis seized in England

| Country of origin | 1979 Number of samples | 1979 THC content (%) Range | 1979 THC content (%) Mean | 1980 Number of samples | 1980 THC content (%) Range | 1980 THC content (%) Mean | 1981 Number of samples | 1981 THC content (%) Range | 1981 THC content (%) Mean |
|---|---|---|---|---|---|---|---|---|---|
| Colombia | 1 | | 6.8 | – | | | 1 | | 8.0 |
| Ghana | – | | | 1 | | 3.4 | – | | |
| Grenada | – | | | – | | | 1 | | 1.8 |
| India | 5[a] | 1.2 – 11 | 3.3 | 3 | 8.4 – 12 | 11 | 2 | 11 – 11 | 11 |
| Jamaica | 14 | 2.1 – 4.2 | 3.0 | 4 | 4.5 – 6.1 | 5.3 | 2 | 4.4 – 5.7 | 5.1 |
| Kenya | 5 | 2.2 – 4.1 | 3.4 | 7 | 1.9 – 5.8 | 3.1 | 4 | 2.3 – 4.2 | 3.4 |
| Malawi | – | | | 1 | | 3.8 | – | | |
| Nigeria | 15 | 2.4 – 8.4 | 4.5 | 6 | 2.4 – 7.7 | 4.9 | 4 | 4.5 – 5.3 | 4.8 |
| South Africa | 10 | 1.3 – 4.2 | 3.1 | 7 | 2.3 – 6.4 | 3.8 | 13 | 2.8 – 7.6 | 4.4 |
| Sri Lanka | 1 | | 1.0 | – | | | 2 | 1.8 – 2.8 | 2.3 |
| Swaziland | 1 | | 3.6 | – | | | 1 | | 3.1 |
| Thailand | 4 | 5.3 – 8.1 | 6.7 | 1 | | 11 | 4 | 2.8 – 12 | 6.1 |
| Uganda | – | | | 1 | | 5.0 | – | | |
| United Republic of Tanzania | 2 | 1.7 – 6.2 | 4.0 | – | | | – | | |
| United States | 1 | | 4.8 | 9 | 0.6 – 8.2 | 2 6 | 2 | 7.2 – 9.7 | 8.5 |
| Zambia | 2 | 2.3 – 7.7 | 5.0 | 1 | | 3.0 | 2 | 1.9 – 5.6 | 3.8 |
| Zimbabwe | 3 | 1.2 – 4.6 | 3.0 | 3 | 1.2—4.1 | 2.4 | 3 | 2.3 – 5.9 | 3.9 |
| Total | 64 | | | 44 | | | 41 | | |

## Total THC content of hashish seized in England

| Country of origin | 1979 Number of samples | 1979 THC content (%) Range | 1979 THC content (%) Mean | 1980 Number of samples | 1980 THC content (%) Range | 1980 THC content (%) Mean | 1981 Number of samples | 1981 THC content (%) Range | 1981 THC content (%) Mean |
|---|---|---|---|---|---|---|---|---|---|
| Egypt | – | | | – | | | 1 | | 11 |
| India | 8 | 5.1 – 18 | 12.5 | – | | | 12 | 3.8 – 21 | 11 |
| Lebanon | 7 | 5.0 – 13 | 8.8 | 2 | 9.1 – 12 | 11 | 5 | 6.1 – 12 | 8.8 |
| Morocco | 2 | 6.8 – 7.1 | 7.0 | 1 | | 8.2 | – | | |
| Nepal | – | | | 1 | | 12 | | | |
| Pakistan | 8 | 3.9 – 13 | 6.0 | 3 | 7.0 – 11 | 8.5 | 6 | 10 – 14 | 12 |
| Turkey | 1 | | 8.7 | 1 | 8.8 | 8.8 | 1 | | 5.8 |
| Total | 26 | | | 8 | | | 25 | | |

## Total THC content of seized cannabis oil[a]

| Country of origin | 1979 Number of samples | 1979 THC content (%) Range | 1979 THC content (%) Mean | 1980 Number of samples | 1980 THC content (%) Range | 1980 THC content (%) Mean | 1981 Number of samples | 1981 THC content (%) Range | 1981 THC content (%) Mean |
|---|---|---|---|---|---|---|---|---|---|
| India | 1 | | 40 | – | | | 2 | 40 – 70 | 55 |
| Jamaica | 1 | | 5.3 | – | | | – | | |
| Lebanon | – | | | 1 | | 23 | 2 | 17 – 19 | 18 |
| Morocco | – | | | – | | | 1 | | 16 |
| Pakistan | 1 | | 39 | 1 | | 42 | – | | |
| Nepal | – | | | – | | | 2 | 20 – 35 | 28 |
| Total | 3 | | | 2 | | | 7 | | |

[a] Manufactured from cannabis resin except sample from Jamaica, which was manufactured from cannabis.

BON 34 (3), 101 (1982)